50 WALKS IN

The Lake District

50 WALKS OF 2–10 MILES

First published 2002
Researched and written by Bil Birkett, John Gillham, Paddy Dillon, Dennis Kelsall,
Terry Marsh, Hugh Taylor and Moira McCrossan
Fully updated 2007
Field checked by Chris Bagshaw

Series Management: Bookwork Creative Associates Ltd
Commissioning Editor: Sandy Draper
Series Editors: Sandy Draper and Marilynne Lanng
Designers: Elizabeth Baldin and Andrew Milne
Picture Research: Liz Stacey
Proofreaders: Suzanne Juby and Pamela Stagg
Cartography provided by the Mapping Services Department of AA Publishing

Produced by AA Publishing
© Automobile Association Developments Limited 2008

Published by AA Publishing (a trading name of Automobile Association Developments Limited,
whose registered office is Fanum House, Basing View, Basingstoke, Hampshire RG21 4EA;
registered number 1878835)

Enabled by [Ordnance Survey] This product includes mapping data licensed from the Ordnance
Survey® with the permission of the Controller of Her Majesty's
Stationery Office. © Crown Copyright 2008. All rights reserved. Licence number 100021153.

A03370

ISBN: 978-0-7495-5595-5

A CIP catalogue record for this book is available from the British Library.

The contents of this book are believed correct at the time of printing. Nevertheless, the publishers cannot be held responsible for any errors or omissions or for changes in the details
given in this book or for the consequences of any reliance on the information it provides.
This does not affect your statutory rights. We have tried to ensure accuracy in this book, but
things do change and we would be grateful if readers would advise us of any inaccuracies they
may encounter.

We have taken all reasonable steps to ensure that these walks are safe and achievable by
walkers with a realistic level of fitness. However, all outdoor activities involve a degree of risk
and the publishers accept no responsibility for any injuries caused to readers whilst following
these walks. For more advice on walking safely see page 144. The mileage range shown on the
front cover is for guidance only – some walks may be less than or exceed these distances.

Visit AA Publishing's website www.theAA.com/travel

Colour reproduction by Keenes Group, Andover
Printed by Printer Trento Srl, Italy

Acknowle[dgements]
The Auto[...]   [...] companies and
picture lib[...]

3 AA/T M[...]   [...] Mackie,
47 AA/T [...]   [...] & N Bonetti,
116/7 AA[...]

Every eff[ort...]   [...]n advance for
an accide[nt...]   [...]ving edition of
this public[ation...]

Mountain (Walk 29)

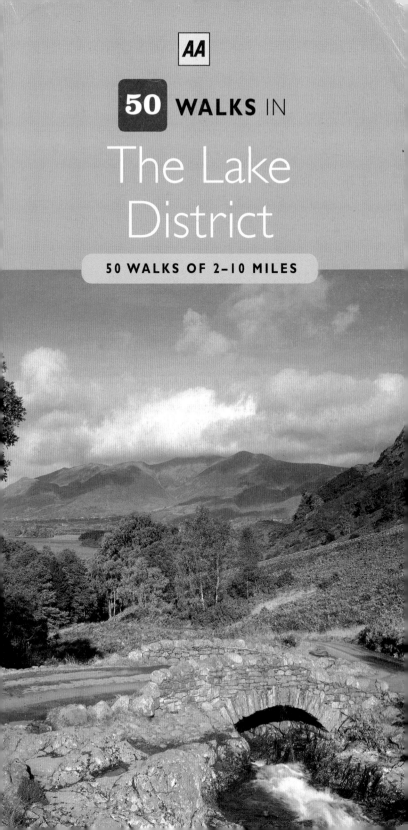

AA

50 WALKS IN

The Lake District

50 WALKS OF 2–10 MILES

Contents

Contents

WALK		RATING	DISTANCE	PAGE

Rating

Each walk is rated for its relative difficulty compared to the other walks in this book. Walks marked +++ are likely to be shorter and easier with little total ascent. The hardest walks are marked +++

Walking in Safety

For advice and safety tips see page 144.

Locator Map

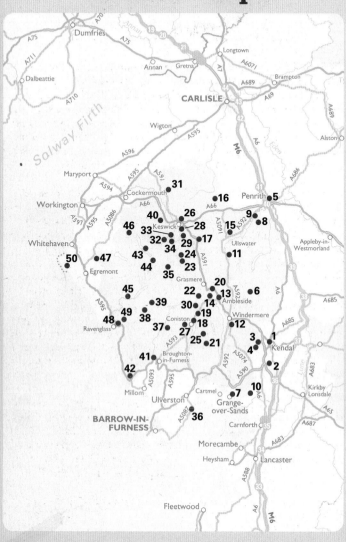

Legend

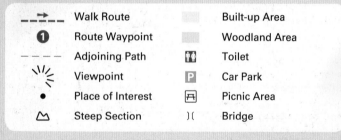

→	Walk Route	▨	Built-up Area
❶	Route Waypoint	▨	Woodland Area
– – –	Adjoining Path	🚻	Toilet
☼	Viewpoint	🅿	Car Park
•	Place of Interest	🛆	Picnic Area
⌂	Steep Section	)(	Bridge

Introducing
the Lake district

The Lake District occupies the south-western corner of Cumbria, one of England's largest counties. At its heart is a series of valleys (dales) cutting through an uplifted button of mountains (fells). This is a glaciated landscape where retreating ice more than 15,000 years ago scooped deep hollows in the valley floors. Filled by becks and rivers, the hollows became the lakes we know today. Much of this region is in England's largest national park. The Lake District National Park Authority protects 885 square miles (2,292sq km) from its headquarters on the outskirts of Kendal.

For many visitors, Bowness-on-Windermere is their first introduction to this area. But if they don't stray far from their tour bus, they will barely catch a glimpse of the real Lake District. This is a landscape seemingly made for exploring on foot. When the great poets of the early 19th century began to popularise its picturesque scenery, they did so from its felltops, from its remote daleheads and mountain becks. They took delight in climbing above the trees, to look down on the silvery lakes and ever-changing light. So escape the tourist bustle of Bowness with a walk on Brant Fell and see Windermere unfold beneath you, ringed by woodlands. While the crowds gape at Wordsworth's grave in Grasmere, you will be closer to the poet's spirit by the quiet shores of Rydal Water or among the shining tarns and tiny crags of Loughrigg. Keswick may seem like a retail park on a summer Saturday, so why not rise above the melée and look down on the town from Walla Crag, Cat Bells or Latrigg.

You will find grand isolation too, on the rounded, grassy northern fells above Bassenthwaite and Mungrisedale. And if you have never ventured to the western Lakes, what breathtaking sights await you. You'll find quiet sides to Coniston and Langdale and, in Dunnerdale, a landscape surely unchanged since Wordsworth's day. Remote Eskdale will enchant and Nannycatch delight even those who think they know this area well.

But there is more to the Lake District than just the area within the National Park boundary. To the south, vast Morecambe Bay is fringed by delightful limestone outcrops, for many holiday-makers, the first glimpses of the mountains still to come. To the north east and far west, red sandstone rises from the green farmland. In the east Penrith Beacon looks out over the Vale of Eden stretching north to the Scottish border, bounded by the formidable profile of Lakeland's eastern fells. To the far west, the cliffs of St Bees look out over the grey Irish Sea.

PUBLIC TRANSPORT

The Lake District is a mixed bag when it comes to public transport. While even the remoter parts may have a bus service, trying to link them up at times when you want to go walking can prove quite a challenge. Trains and community buses complete the network and regular service buses link the main towns, but don't expect to catch one much after 6pm. For more information and a timetable call the county's information line on 0871 200 2233 or visit the website www.traveline.info

These walks were originally compiled in the aftermath of 2001's tragic foot and mouth epidemic, in which thousands of Cumbria's livestock were slaughtered. Some access restrictions were still in place, particularly in the north and east of the county. The choice of walks reflects that restriction to a certain extent. Revisiting the walks for this revision, it is striking how well the countryside has recovered from those grim days. The distinctive fell breeds of sheep – Rough Fell, Herdwick, Swaledale are still familiar companions and you'll find the Lakeland landscape is as varied on these walks as many counties can claim in their entirety. So whether you're drawn by the literary connections, the breathtaking views, the quiet sylvan corners or the majesty of lonely fellsides, you will not be disappointed.

Using this book

INFORMATION PANELS

An information panel for each walk shows its relative difficulty (see Walk 5), the distance and total amount of ascent. An indication of the gradients you will encounter is shown by the rating ▲▲▲ (no steep slopes) to ▲▲▲ (several very steep slopes).

MAPS

There are 30 maps, covering 40 of the walks. Some walks have a suggested option in the same area. The information panel for these walks will tell you how much extra walking is involved. On short-cut suggestions the panel will tell you the total distance if you set out from the start of the main walk. Where an option returns to the same point on the main walk, just the distance of the loop is given. Where an option leaves the main walk at one point and returns to it at another, then the distance shown is for the whole walk. The minimum time suggested is for reasonably fit walkers and doesn't allow for stops. Each walk has a suggested Ordnance Survey map.

START POINTS

The start of each walk is given as a six-figure grid reference prefixed by two letters indicating which 100-km square of the National Grid it refers to. You'll find more information on grid references on most Ordnance Survey maps.

DOGS

We have tried to give dog owners useful advice about how dog friendly each walk is. Please respect other countryside users. Keep your dog under control, especially around livestock, and obey local bylaws and other dog control notices.

CAR PARKING

Many of the car parks suggested are public, but occasionally you may find you have to park on the roadside or in a lay-by. Please be considerate when you leave your car, ensuring that access roads or gates are not blocked and that other vehicles can pass safely.

Right: Pooley Bridge Boathouse, on the shores of Ullswater (Walk 8)

Kendal's Two Castles

Visit two ancient castles, on opposite banks of the River Kent.

WALK 1

DISTANCE 3 miles (4.8km)   **MINIMUM TIME** 1hr 30min

ASCENT/GRADIENT 300ft (91m) ▲▲▲   **LEVEL OF DIFFICULTY** ✦✦✦

PATHS Pavements, surfaced and grassy paths with steps, no stiles

LANDSCAPE Historic townscape and parkland

SUGGESTED MAP OS Explorer OL7 The English Lakes (SE)

START / FINISH Grid reference: SD 518928

DOG FRIENDLINESS Parkland popular but busy roads through town

PARKING Free parking area by river (occasionally occupied by fairground), numerous pay car parks near by

PUBLIC TOILETS Near road bridge, Miller Bridge, end of river parking area

---

Known as the 'Auld Grey Town', because of the colour of its predominantly limestone buildings, enterprising Kendal retains much of its original character. Until recently Kendal was the administrative centre for the former county of Westmorland. Sited either side of the River Kent, its occupation stretches from Roman times to the present day and its varied stone buildings, nooks, crannies, yards and castles offer a rich historical tapestry. This walk visits two important strongholds located strategically on high ground either side of the river; Kendal Castle and Castle Howe.

Kendal Castle

Sited in a commanding position over Kendal and the River Kent, the ruined Kendal Castle is quietly impressive and offers fine views in all directions. The people of Kendal know it as an old friend and may tell you that this was the birthplace of Catherine Parr who became Henry VIII's sixth and last wife in 1543. Although her grandfather, William Parr who died in 1483, lies entombed in Kendal parish church, apparently there is no evidence that Catherine ever set foot in Kendal and the castle was probably already falling into decay by that time.

It is thought that Kendal Castle succeeded Castle Howe, sited opposite on the western side of the river, sometime in the late 12th century. After the Norman barons had secured the kingdom they required quarters with sufficient space to administer their feudal territories and so replaced their wooden motte-and-bailey castles with castles of stone. Timber buildings surrounded by a ditch and small tower were replaced by new stone buildings in about 1220 and work continued until 1280 by one of the early barons of Kendal, either Gilbert Fitzrheinfred or his son William de Lancaster.

Today, the ruins of Kendal Castle consist of a circular defensive wall and three towers plus a residential gatehouse surrounded by a partly filled ditch. The entrance path leads through the wall at the point where a gatehouse once stood. To the left are the largest standing remains, the house where the baron's family lived, known as the Lyons Den, or Machell Tower. To the right, a favourite climb for adventurous children, stands the Troutbeck Tower sporting its 'dungeon room' below and garderobe (toilet), with free fall into the ditch/moat, above. If you do climb the tower, and it may be against regulations to do so, take care not to fall through the unprotected hole. It could be very dangerous and embarrassing. South of the compound is a lesser tower and the exit here, a former gatehouse, is now barred by a locked door.

The Parr family occupied the castle for four generations, from 1380 to 1486, when William Parr's widow remarried and moved to Northamptonshire. The castle fell into ruin and much of the stone is thought to have been recycled for use in building works in the 'Auld Grey Town' below.

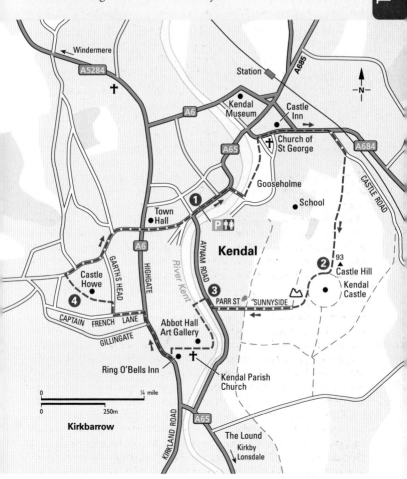

WALK 1 DIRECTIONS

❶ Walk upstream along the riverside parking area to a footbridge crossing the river. Cross and bear left to follow the surfaced walkway, through Gooseholme. At the junction of roads beyond the Church of St George turn right down Castle Street. Pass the Castle Inn and

Ann Street, keeping right and continuing up the hill to Castle Road on the right. Ascend Castle Road to where a kissing gate on the right leads on to Castle Hill. Follow the broad path up the hill to the ruins of Kendal Castle.

❷ Round the castle ruins until, at a point beneath its southern end, a path can be found dropping down

WALK 1

to the right. Descend steeply to pass through an iron kissing gate on to Sunnyside. Go down the road over the old canal bridge and emerge on Aynam Road.

WHAT TO LOOK OUT FOR

Castle Howe, Kendal's first Norman motte-and-bailey castle, was built between 1068 and 1100. At the time it was the cutting northern edge of the rapidly established Norman kingdom and Kendal, then known as Kirkbie Strickland, was mentioned in the Domesday survey of 1086. The obelisk on top of Castle Howe was designed by Francis Webster and built by William Holme in 1778. It was dedicated to the 'Glorious Revolution' of 1688 when William of Orange replaced James II. It is known locally as 'Bill Holmes' bodkin'.

❸ Turn right along Aynam Road to a crossing. Cross and find a footbridge leading over the River Kent. Over the river bear left, downstream, and walk past Abbot Hall to a narrow, surfaced path leading right. Take this path, lined by yew trees and limestone coping stones, to pass between Kendal parish church and Abbot Hall Art Gallery. Emerge on to the Kirkland Road, the main road through Kendal, by the impressive iron gates of the church with the Ring O'Bells pub to the left. Turn right along the road and proceed 150yds (137m) to a crossing. Cross it then bear right to cross

WHERE TO EAT AND DRINK

Kendal is famed for its many fine pubs and there is a plethora of cafés and restaurants. On this walk you pass the Castle Inn and the Ring O'Bells. Both offer real ale and bar meals. In Kirkland there are several fish and chip shops and take-aways. The Brewery Arts Centre, just beyond Captain French Lane along Highgate, has both café and bar facilities.

Gillingate and keep along the main road, now called Highgate. At Lightfoot's chemist shop go left up Captain French Lane for 300yds (274m), then right up Garths Head. Follow this until a steep path ascends to the left. Steps lead to a terrace and a view out over Kendal. Cross the grass terrace towards the mound and its distinct bodkin-shaped obelisk. Climb the steps then spiral left until, as the path levels, steps lead up to the right to the obelisk and the top of Castle Howe.

❹ Return to the path and go right. Find a gap on the left and emerge on the road at the top of Beast Banks. Descend the hill, which becomes Allhallows Lane, to the traffic lights and pedestrian crossing opposite the Town Hall. Cross the road and go left and then immediately right down Lowther Street. Go left at the bottom to a zebra crossing beyond the Holy Trinity of St George, which leads to the riverside.

WHILE YOU'RE THERE

Kendal Museum, Abbot Hall Art Gallery and Kendal parish church are all centres of attraction. The former, has everything from stuffed bears and crocodiles to neolithic Langdale stone axes. There are so many interesting buildings and features in Kendal, the history so rich and varied, it is impossible to single out individual items. Have a roam and afterwards know that there are numerous quiet places on the banks of the River Kent, reputedly England's fastest flowing river, to eat your fish and chips.

Gunpowder, Sedgwick and the Lancaster Canal

In the 18th century engineers tunnelled through a hill to bring the Lancaster Canal past a gunpowder factory.

DISTANCE 5.5 miles (8.8km) **MINIMUM TIME** 2hrs 30min

ASCENT/GRADIENT 600ft (183m) ▲▲▲ **LEVEL OF DIFFICULTY** +++

PATHS Field paths, tow paths and some quiet lanes, 10 stiles

LANDSCAPE Grazing fields cover rolling landscape, distant hills

SUGGESTED MAP OS Explorer OL7 The English Lakes (SE)

START / FINISH Grid reference: SD 513870

DOG FRIENDLINESS On lead along lanes and where livestock are grazing

PARKING Roadside parking in Sedgwick

PUBLIC TOILETS None en route

The 18th century saw the beginnings of industrialisation in Britain, when machines were invented that performed the labour of umpteen people. Nowhere was the transformation more startling than in the textile industries, where large, water-powered mills replaced an age-old tradition of home working. Mechanisation affected other areas too, but the limiting factor to expansion was transport. Factories which were located beside navigable water could trade by boat, but the fast-flowing rivers and streams powering the new machinery lay far inland, accessible only by packhorses or lumbering carts. A second revolution came with the development of canals, which effectively took the seaboard into the heart of the countryside. Now serviced by cheap and speedy transport, the areas they reached profited from burgeoning new industries.

A New Age

Kendal had long been a successful town, flourishing from the woollen and other industries, but remoteness from the main population and industrial centres became an increasing threat to prosperity. Although the canal age dawned in the mid-1750s with the Sankey Brook and Worsley canals, it was not until 1792 that a waterway linking Kendal to the industrial heartland of Lancashire via Lancaster and Preston was sanctioned. By 1797, barges were passing between Tewitfield and Preston, and a tramway across the Ribble later gave access to the south. The final section was this stretch into Kendal, routed via Sedgwick to serve the gunpowder factories beside the River Kent.

The Hincaster Tunnel

However, blocking the way was a hill, and the only means of avoiding a lengthy detour was to burrow straight through. Completed in 1817, the Hincaster Tunnel is 378yds (346m) long and, as you will see, remains a magnificent feat of engineering. To minimise expense, the tunnel did not include a tow path but, instead, barges were pulled through by hand using a fixed cable or 'legged' by the bargees. Further obstacles lay in river and other crossings, two of which are passed on this ramble.

SEDGWICK

Although the aqueduct across Stainton Beck is hardly apparent from above, it is no less an achievement than the skew aqueduct at Sedgwick, where the walk begins. Have a look at its stonework as you pass beneath. A traditional arch would have had to extend over the full width of the crossing if it were not to lose its inherent strength. But, by laying the courses at an angle, the integrity of the structure was retained, allowing the span to be matched to the crossing. The result, I'm sure you'll agree, is as aesthetically pleasing as it is practical.

Commercial traffic ended in 1947, and the northern stretch was de-watered in 1955, with more sections disappearing beneath the M6 motorway and Kendal bypass. However, what remains is full of interest and beauty, and a delight to explore.

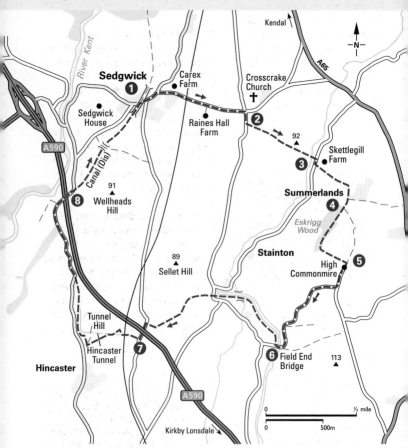

WALK 2 DIRECTIONS

1 From the canal aqueduct, follow the Natland lane as far as the second junction by Carex Farm and turn right. At Crosscrake church, go right again, signed 'Stainton Cross'.

2 Leave through the first gate on the left and cross to a stile in the far right corner of the field. Follow the left-hand hedge, continuing upwards over a second stile. Beyond the crest, drop to Skettlegill Farm, cross Stainton Beck and walk to the lane beyond.

3 Cross to a gate opposite between buildings and then pass through another gate ahead. Climb again to a stile, and maintain your direction across the next field. Over another stile, walk to the far wall and turn right to the corner before emerging on to a track by Summerlands.

4 Walk down the track, passing through a gate by Eskrigg Wood. The way shortly broadens into a meadow, but keep going to the further of two gates at the left corner. A waymark confirms the route along a hedged track into rough woodland. Soon the path bends left to a stile near a gate. Walk away across a field to a track at the far side.

5 Follow the track to the right, leading through a small, gated farmyard at High Commonmire, and continuing beyond as a metalled way. Bear right at a junction and carry on down to Field End Bridge.

6 Cross the canal, drop left on to the tow path and walk beneath the bridge. Presently, beyond an aqueduct built to take the waterway over Stainton Beck, the canal ends, the onward section to Kendal has been been filled in, de-watered or lost beneath road construction. However, its course remains clear, eventually leading to a lane below the A590.

7 Pass under the bridge and rejoin the canal through a gate on the right. A cutting leads to the mouth of the Hincaster Tunnel, where a path to the left carries walkers, as it once did horses, over Tunnel Hill. At the far side, turn right behind some cottages to regain the tow path. Remain by the canal until forced on to the lane and continue eventually to cross the A590.

8 Just beyond the bridge, steps rise to a field on the right. Walk ahead beside the fence, and on across the field, eventually passing beneath a lone bridge. Beyond, the canal cutting is again evident, accompanying you to Sedgwick, where steps beside the aqueduct drop to the road.

Along the Limestone of Cunswick Scar

The freedom of the heights, extensive views and varied flora, fauna and fossils make this an intriguing and liberating outing.

DISTANCE *3 miles (4.8km)* MINIMUM TIME *1hr 30min*

ASCENT/GRADIENT *250ft (79m)* ▲▲▲ LEVEL OF DIFFICULTY +++

PATHS *Paths and tracks, can be muddy, take care as edge of scar is unguarded in places, 2 stiles*

LANDSCAPE *Fields and open fell along high limestone shoulder*

SUGGESTED MAP *OS Explorer OL7 The English Lakes (SE)*

START / FINISH *Grid reference: SD 489923*

DOG FRIENDLINESS *Fellside grazed by sheep, dogs must be under control*

PARKING *Beneath radio mast near top of hill*

PUBLIC TOILETS *None en route; nearest in Kendal*

At the south-western boundary of the Lake District National Park, Cunswick Scar is a high shoulder of white Carboniferous limestone running north to south. Its southern end links with Scout Scar, though a geological fault, taken by the high Underbarrow Road, has displaced the whole of Scout Scar westwards from the northern leg of Cunswick Scar and Cunswick Fell. From the east, gently sloping fellside rises to a height of 680ft (207m), before suddenly falling in a vertical face to present a long and spectacular cliff running above the woods and pastures of Underbarrow. The effect is dramatic and the tops of both Cunswick Scar and Scout Scar present wonderful views over Kentdale and the Lyth Valley, extending outwards to the Lakeland fells, Morecambe Bay and the distant hills of Yorkshire.

Carboniferous Limestone

The naked white bones of both these scars are composed of pure Carboniferous limestone. This attractive alkaline rock, which has provided the building material for most of the nearby town of Kendal, is home to a rich flora and fauna and noted for its splendid fossils. It was formed some 270–350 million years ago when a warm shallow sea covered the central dome of Lakeland. Living in its waters were corals, brachiopods (shellfish), molluscs, gastropods (snails) and colonies of crinoids – sometimes referred to as sea lilies. The shell-like remains of these animals sank to the bottom of the seabed and, over the aeons, accumulated into thick layers or beds. These beds compacted together and solidified to form the brilliant white Carboniferous limestone we see exposed today.

By the end of the Carboniferous period the Lake District was buried under several thousand feet of limestone. A period of uplifting and folding, followed by arid desert conditions, stripped down through the limestone layers until, finally, the glaciation of the Ice Age (the last glacial retreat ending around 15,000 years ago) gouged, shattered and polished Cunswick Scar principally into the outline shape we see now. The more recent effects of freeze and thaw shattering has added the banks of scree seen to the west, beneath the scar.

CUNSWICK SCAR

The dissolving action of carbolic acid, produced by endless rainwater, has resulted in the columns (clints) and deep vertical fissures (grykes) of the limestone pavements along the top of the scar.

The west face of the scar, overlooking the mixed woods, emerald fields, and the scattered white farmsteads of the Lyth and Underbarrow valleys, contrasts markedly with the starkness of the plateau above. On these cliffs, alongside the tenacious yew and pine, which have forced their way into secure rocky crannies, brightly coloured flowers abound in summertime. In June the prevailing colour of these flowers is yellow. Spreads of common rock rose, hoary rock rose, horseshoe vetch and hawkweeds drape across the rock ledges and look particularly striking against the grey whiteness of the limestone and the dark green foliage of the yew.

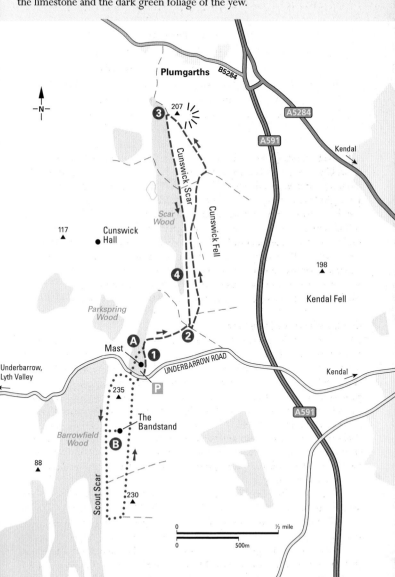

WALK 3 DIRECTIONS

1 Walk away from the road, cross the sloping limestone bed that forms the car park and take the track that leads to the communications mast. Pass a low barrier then bear right to follow the narrow path through the wood. Leave the wood by a kissing gate at the junction of the stone walls. Look for a footpath sign 'Cunswick Fell'. Enter the field and continue by the stone wall. On reaching the corner of the field go right and follow the path parallel to the wall. Continue over the humpback of the field and drop to pass a gate, beyond which the wall turns a sharp corner.

WHILE YOU'RE THERE

To the west of the scar the quiet Underbarrow and Lyth valleys are worthy of exploration. The Lyth Valley particularly is noted for its damson trees. The damson is a form of small plum. In springtime its white blossom resembles winter snows and in autumn its annual harvest often used for jam or wine making.

2 Continue ahead on a grassy path for 30yds (27m) then follow it round to the left, aiming for a lone fingerpost. Ignore the right turn and stay with the track over the brow and down to a gate in a fence. Go through the gate and follow the wall on the right as it descends to a dip and round to the right. Beyond the dip, a path traces off left to join a more prominent track. Turn left on this and follow it to the top of the hill where you'll find the summit cairn of Cunswick Scar, a commanding viewpoint.

3 Walk on beyond the cairn and drop to the lower terrace edged by the scar. Take care here, the cliff face of the scar is unfenced at this point and reaches a vertical height of around 40ft (12m). Turn left, facing out, and bear south along the edge of the scar. A fence now runs along the edge of the crag. Keep along the rim of the scar through an avenue of gorse and hazel to the edge of a wall. Take the narrow path alongside the wall to find a stile crossing the fence.

WHERE TO EAT AND DRINK

Kendal is near by and offers a huge choice. Underbarrow and the Lyth Valley lie to the east and there are a number of quaint little inns that offer bar meals. Nearest to the scar are the Punch Bowl inns at Underbarrow and Crosthwaite.

4 Cross the stile and continue by the wall before bearing left to merge with the original footpath at the end of the raised shoulder. Retrace your steps to join the dry-stone wall at its corner, with the gate just beyond. Pass the gate and follow the path along by the walls to the kissing gate at the edge of the wood. Follow the path left through the wood.

WHAT TO LOOK OUT FOR

There are many fossils in the limestone of Cunswick Scar and Cunswick Fell. Particularly attractive are the corals, and there are at least three varieties to be found. The largest of these is the colonial coral which may form clumps of up to 1ft (30cm) in diameter. Molluscs are well represented and gastropods (snails) are abundant. Sometimes it is the hard calcium shell of the snail that has been preserved. On other occasions it is the spiralling softer inner-body of the snail that remains.

Along Scout Scar

Open limestone scar leads along an exposed edge with a fine aspect.

See map and information panel for Walk 3

WALK 4

DISTANCE 4.5 miles (7.2km) **MINIMUM TIME** 2hrs 15min

ASCENT/GRADIENT 361ft (110m) ▲▲▲ **LEVEL OF DIFFICULTY** ✦✦✦

WALK 4 DIRECTIONS (Walk 3 option)

To extend Walk 3 don't bear left through the wood on your return journey, but follow a little path going right at Point **Ⓐ** to pass the fenced compound of the communications mast on its right side. Beyond this the path emerges on to the unprotected rim of an old quarry. Care is required as the 40ft (12m) drop into the car park below is unmarked and unfenced. Bear left and then walk down to the Underbarrow Road. Go right down the road until an iron kissing gate opens to the left.

Pass through the gate and follow the well-defined polished stony path rising through the thorn trees and mixed woods to the right. The path ascends to the northern tip of Scout Scar. There is now a choice of ways, both of which lead due south along the scar. The broad path goes inland away from the rim of the scar while a well-defined path traverses the edge of the scar itself. The outward path gives the most satisfying views though it is totally unprotected and steep cliffs, up to 70ft (21m) high, fall directly below.

A path climbs left up to Point **Ⓑ**, the unmistakable walled shelter topped by a circular concrete dome. Know locally by various names: 'The Bandstand', 'The Mushroom' and 'The Umbrella', the shelter is sited on a commanding viewpoint. A depiction of the Lakeland fells is marked on its inner rim. The shelter was built in 1912 as a memorial to King George V and it has been restored a few times. From the shelter walk south until a wall cuts across the scar.

At this point bear left along the wall and follow it eastwards over the crest of the scar. At the junction with the field wall, defining the eastern edge of the shoulder, go left. Head north following the path parallel to the wall. Continue along this path until it falls through thorn bushes to rejoin the original route by the kissing gate. Regain the road and ascend to the top of the hill to return to the car park.

WHAT TO LOOK OUT FOR

Along the top of Scout Scar you can see the limestone pavement of deep vertical fissures (grykes) formed by weathering, which separate the more resistant limestone columns (clints). The deeper grykes provide moist, sheltered conditions for rare plants, including ferns, to flourish.

On Penrith Beacon

Walk in the footsteps of Jacobites from the rebellions of 1715 and 1745.

WALK 5

DISTANCE *3 miles (4.8km)*   MINIMUM TIME *2hrs*

ASCENT/GRADIENT *360ft (110m)* ▲▲▲   LEVEL OF DIFFICULTY ✦✦✦

PATHS *Good paths and pavements, no stiles*

LANDSCAPE *Town and woodland*

SUGGESTED MAP *OS Explorer OL5 The English Lakes (NE)*

START / FINISH *Grid reference: NY 517307*

DOG FRIENDLINESS *This is where locals walk their dogs*

PARKING *Car park at bus station*

PUBLIC TOILETS *At car park*

WALK 5 DIRECTIONS

Beacons were a means of communication in the past. Great fires lit on prominent hills would warn the surrounding community and watchers on far-off hillsides of approaching danger. In the case of Penrith the danger was usually a raid by the Scots. They ransacked the town on several occasions, the last being in 1745.

In an attempt to restore James Stuart (1688–1766), the 'Old Pretender', to the throne as James III, the Jacobites rose in 1715 and marched south with an army of Highlanders. Joined by the Earl of Derwentwater and 'a parcel of Northcountry jockeys and foxhunters' at Brampton, they advanced on Penrith. Beacons were fired and the Cumberland and Westmorland militia called out. Accompanied by several thousand yeomen, farmers and labourers they marched to intercept the Jacobite forces at Penrith Fell. However, when they encountered the advance guard, the defending army ran away leaving their commanders, Lord Lonsdale and Bishop Nicholson to fend for themselves. Lonsdale fled to Appleby and the bishop's coachman drove his master home to Rose Castle. The Jacobites levied a contribution of £500 on Penrith but otherwise left it undisturbed. They did, however, plunder Lowther Hall. The rebellion ended in failure and Derwentwater had his estates forfeited and his head chopped off.

This walk begins at the bus station car park in Penrith. Exit to Sandgate and turn left, cross the double mini-roundabout and continue up Fell Lane to Beacon

WHILE YOU'RE THERE

Acorn Bank Garden and Watermill is a National Trust property at Temple Sowerby. The garden is protected by oak trees and you can walk through the orchards and by the mixed borders. It has the largest collection of herbs in the North and there's a woodland walk leading to the watermill, which is under restoration but open.

WHAT TO LOOK OUT FOR

Penrith has many wonderful and unusual buildings. Sandgate Hall is a 17th-century town house, unaltered since it was built apart from the modern windows. Potter's Lodge, on the corner of Fell Lane and Scaws Drive, is a fine example of Georgian architecture.

Edge. Cross the road, go through a gate and follow the path up through the trees where it veers left, passing a gate on your right. The path turns sharp right into a dog-leg at a second gate and then left at another gate to the right. Continue from here, passing a path forking off to the right, and in 100yds (91m) arrive at Beacon Pike. There's a view from here over Penrith and beyond it to the fells in the west.

Following the defeat of the 1715 rebellion Penrith enjoyed 30 years of relative peace. Then the Jacobites struck again and this time at their head came James' son, Prince Charles Edward (1720–88), the 'Young Pretender' or 'Bonnie' Prince Charlie. He had sailed from France with a party of supporters and raised his standard at Glenfinnan in the Scottish Highlands. He marched south, with an army of Highlanders, taking Carlisle and by 18 November the advance party arrived in Penrith where they met no opposition. On the 22 November the prince arrived and took up quarters at 19 Devonshire Street. The Jacobites requisitioned 1,000 stone (6,350kg) of hay and ten cartloads of oats from Lowther Hall, Dalemain, Eden Hall, Hutton John, Hutton Hall and Greystoke Castle. The rebel army got as far as Derby but indecisiveness delayed them and eventually they

turned back. Penrith Beacon was lit again to call the countryside to arms. News that they were in retreat encouraged people to turn out to cut off the stragglers. On 15 December at Langwathby, a Penrith party defeated 110 of the Jacobite's Hussars. For this 'Sunday Huntin' the main Jacobite army threatened to burn Penrith. Later that day Highland troops, under Lord George Murray, defeated a Hanoverian force at Clifton Moor. Murray joined the prince at Penrith, ready to leave for the long march north to eventual defeat.

From Beacon Pike retrace your route to the fork passed earlier and turn left on to the grassy path through the woods. When you encounter another locked gate across the path, veer slightly left and follow the line of the fence, skirting Beacon Hill, until it rejoins the original route. Return to Beacon Edge, turn right and follow the road to a path ('Salkeld Road'). Turn right and follow it along the back of the cemetery.

The footpath goes through a couple of gates before arriving at the golf course. Cross the fairways then turn left down Salkeld Road, turning left again at its junction with Beacon Edge. Turn right and go down Wordsworth Street, turn left into Meeting House Lane and finally right, back into Sandgate.

WHERE TO EAT AND DRINK

The Agricultural Hotel in Castlegate, next to Morrison's, is one of the great pubs of Cumbria. Warm and friendly it serves a wide variety of pub grub including local specialities like black pudding and mash with a Dijon mustard sauce. You can wash it down with a pint of Jennings ale.

Exploring Upper Kentmere

Once ravaged by Scottish reivers, this lovely remote valley now basks in enviable tranquillity.

WALK 6

DISTANCE 6.75 miles (10.9km)   **MINIMUM TIME** 2hrs 15min

ASCENT/GRADIENT 689ft (210m) ▲▲▲ **LEVEL OF DIFFICULTY** ✦✦✦

PATHS *Generally good tracks and paths, some open fields, 7 stiles*

LANDSCAPE *Glacial valley, flood meadows, quarry workings and reservoir*

SUGGESTED MAP *OS Explorer OL7 The English Lakes (SE)*

START / FINISH *Grid reference: SD 456040*

DOG FRIENDLINESS *Farmyards and grazing land, so dogs mostly on lead*

PARKING *Very limited in Kentmere, but small field by Low Bridge is occasionally available*

PUBLIC TOILETS *None en route; nearest at Staveley*

From its source, high on the slopes of Mardale Ill Bell at the heart of Cumbria's eastern fells, the River Kent begins a journey through Kentmere, one of the country's loveliest valleys. Deep and narrow, it follows a gently sinuous course south for some 9 miles (14.5km) before breaking free to meander between the rolling hills beyond Staveley. In its higher reaches, the Kent is isolated from frenetic modern life, and there is a wonderful sense of remoteness as you wander below towering crags.

From earliest times, the dale has supported small communities who made a living by farming the confined valley bottoms and lower slopes. Perhaps the pickings were never very great, but it must still have been a tempting target for raiders (known as reivers) from the north, who could ride over the pass from Mardale, grab what livestock or other prizes they might find, and be away again before an alarm could be raised.

Kentmere Hall

The hall at Kentmere was built by the Gilpins around the 14th century, a square, battlemented tower rising over a vaulted basement. A narrow spiral staircase was the only access to the upper floors, a further obstacle to any aggressor who managed to burst through the heavily barred door. With their cattle and sheep safely inside, the family could easily defend themselves.

The troubled times across the North continued after the defeat of the Scots at Flodden in 1513, and it was not until James VI of Scotland succeeded to the English throne almost 100 years later that the raiding way of life ended. However, some security must have been felt before then, since a farmhouse was added in the 16th century and the tower became an outhouse or barn.

Some of the hall's occupants have earned a reputation extending far beyond the lonely valley. Hugh Herd, who acquired the title of the 'Cork Lad of Kentmere', was a giant of a man. Born to a nun at Furness Abbey, he became a champion wrestler and served King Edward VI, in repelling invaders across the border with Scotland. Perhaps less deserving of praise was Richard Gilpin, who is said to have killed the last wild boar in England.

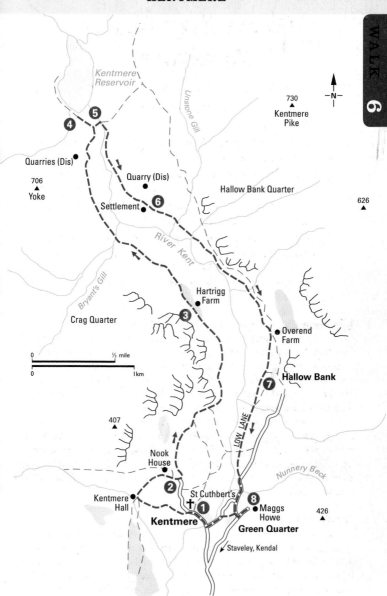

WALK 6 DIRECTIONS

1 Begin on a bridleway, marked 'Kentmere Hall', opposite St Cuthbert's Church. Approach the farmyard, bear right behind cattle pens, then right through a side gate. A signpost, 'Garburn and Reservoir', directs you up the field. Leave at the top and walk to a gate. Pass a barn and go through a gap to another gate, where a track leads past Nook House.

2 Ignore the turn-off to Garburn, and immediately after the next house, Greenhead, go left. Still following signs to the reservoir, bear right through a gate, and then right again at a

WHILE YOU'RE THERE

The present village church dates mainly from the mid-19th century, when the expanding quarries brought new people into the valley. It is dedicated to Cuthbert, a 7th-century Northumbrian saint. Originally buried at Lindisfarne, the monks removed his relics after Vikings destroyed the abbey and the community wandered the North for over a century, perhaps stopping here awhile, before finally laying his body to rest at Durham.

second fork to join a metalled track leading up the valley.

3 The valley bottom is wide and flat. Bear left past the entrance to Hartrigg Farm and continue on a track through the valley, now progressively squeezed between the craggy breasts of Yoke and Kentmere Pike. Eventually the dam appears, rising above the heaps of abandoned slate quarries.

4 Continue to the dam. Fed by waters from two boulder-strewn combes that divide the valley head, the reservoir is a wild and deserted place. But when the sun shines it is a place to linger, and you might glimpse one of the golden eagles that nest near by.

WHAT TO LOOK OUT FOR

Although stone had long been taken for local building, quarrying only became commercially viable after the railway reached Staveley in 1847. The valley has a vein of fine Westmorland slate, and the next 50 years saw the industry expand with eight separate quarries being worked at one time. However, after 1918 cheaper slate from Wales and abroad eroded the markets, and the last workings finally closed in 1956.

5 Bridges below the dam take the return route across the outflows to a path just above, which then follows the windings of the Kent downstream. Beyond the quarries, cross a ladder stile into an enclosure. Leave by a gate on the left by a barn.

6 A track continues through successive valley-bottom fields, eventually leading to Overend Farm. Ignore the tarmac lane and bear right through a gate on to a grass track. Where a track later drops from Hallow Bank, keep ahead along Low Lane.

WHERE TO EAT AND DRINK

Maggs Howe, near the end of the walk, is open daily from lunchtime, serving delicious home-made snacks and cakes. For a pub, you'll have to go back down to Staveley, where both the Eagle and Child and the Duke William welcome families and serve bar meals. There's a good chippy too, open for lunches and teas from Tuesday to Saturday.

7 This delightful old track, its walls luxuriant with mosses and ferns, ultimately emerges on to a lane. Carry on, at the next junction, to a waymarked stile on the right a little further along. The route now lies across the field but, for a snack, continue along the lane to a second junction and turn left to Maggs Howe, above the lane on the right.

8 Retrace your steps to the stile and walk down to the far bottom corner of the field. A steep path drops beside a stream through larch to emerge on to a lane. Turn left and, at the end, go right, to return to to the church.

Over Hampsfell Above Grange-over-Sands

A walk through mixed woods and over open fell above a charming seaside resort.

DISTANCE 4 miles (6.4km)	**MINIMUM TIME** 2hrs
ASCENT/GRADIENT 790ft (241m) ▲▲▲	**LEVEL OF DIFFICULTY** ✦✦✦

PATHS Paths and tracks, can be muddy in places, 7 stiles

LANDSCAPE Town, woods and open fell, extensive seascapes

SUGGESTED MAP OS Explorer OL7 The English Lakes (SE)

START / FINISH Grid reference: SD 410780

DOG FRIENDLINESS Busy lanes and open fell grazed by sheep

PARKING Car park below road and tourist office in central Grange

PUBLIC TOILETS At Ornamental Gardens, north end of car park

TAKE NOTICE
All persons visiting this 'hospice' by permission
Of the owner, are requested to respect private
Property, and not by acts of wanton mischief
And destruction show that they possess more
Muscle than brain. I have no hope that this
Request will be attended to, for as Solomon
Says 'Though thou shouldest bray a
A fool in a mortar among wheat with
A pestle, yet will not his foolishness
Depart from him'.

So reads one of the panels inside the peculiar Hospice of Hampsfell at the high point of this walk. Its tone matches that of Grange-over-Sands, with its neat and tidy white limestone buildings, colourful gardens, sunny aspect and seaside disposition. It has long been a popular seaside resort, particularly since the arrival of the Furness Railway in the town in 1857. Day-trippers would also arrive by steamer via the waters of Morecambe Bay. They disembarked at the Claire House Pier, which was dramatically blown away by a storm in 1928.

Today the sea is somewhat distanced from the sea wall and the town, despite past popularity, has fallen from grace with many holiday-makers and now retains a refined air of quiet dignity. Grange has many fine and interesting buildings and its ornamental gardens, complete with ponds, provide suitable solitude in which to relax and enjoy a picnic. The gardens rise to the open airy spaces of Hampsfell (Hampsfield Fell on the map) via the charming mixed woods of Eggerslack, which add yet another dimension to this pleasant area.

The Hospice of Hampsfell

Built of dressed limestone blocks the neat square tower, around 20ft (6m) high, which adorns the top of Hampsfield Fell is known as the Hospice of Hampsfell. It was apparently built by a minister from nearby Cartmel Priory

GRANGE-OVER-SANDS

over a century ago for 'the shelter and entertainment of travellers over the fell'. Enclosed by a fence of chains supported by small stone pillars to keep cattle out, and with an entrance door and three windows, it provides a convenient shelter should the weather take a turn for the worse. On its north face stone steps guarded by an iron handrail provide access to the top of the tower and a resplendent view.

On the top, a novel direction indicator, consisting of a wooden sighting arrow mounted on a rotating circular table, lets you know which distant point of interest you are looking at. Simply align the arrow to the chosen subject, read the angle created by the arrow and locate it on the list on the east rail.

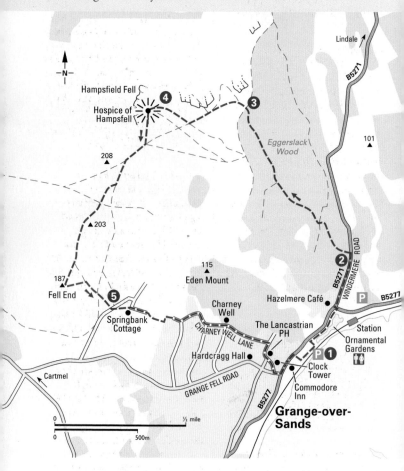

WALK 7 DIRECTIONS

1 Join the main road through Grange and go right (heading north), to pass the ornamental gardens. Cross the road and continue along the pavement to the roundabout. Go left along Windermere Road rising to round the bend, and find steps up to a squeeze stile on the left, signed 'Routon Well/Hampsfield'.

2 Take the path rising through Eggerslack Wood. Cross directly over a surfaced track and continue to pass a house on the left. Steps lead on to a track. Cross this diagonally to follow a track, signed 'Hampsfell'. The track zig-zags to the right (with a house to the left) and continues up through the woods to a stile over the wall.

3 Cross the stile to leave the wood and follow the path directly up the hillside. Pass sections of limestone pavement and little craggy outcrops until the path levels and bears left to a stile over a stone wall. Cross the stile and go right along the wall. Continue in the same direction, following a grassy track, to pass ancient stone cairns and up to the obvious square tower landmark of the Hospice of Hampsfell.

4 Leave the tower, head south and follow the path over the edge of a little limestone escarpment (take care here). Continue over another escarpment and descend to find a stile over the wall. Descend to the bottom of the dip and rise directly up the green hill beyond. Cross over the top and descend to find a stile over the wall. Although the path bears

diagonally left at this point it is usual to continue directly to the little cairn marking Fell End, with fine views over the estuary. Turn sharp left and descend to pick up a grassy track leading left round a little valley of thorn bushes to a gate leading out on to a road.

5 Cross the road, take the squeeze stile and descend diagonally left across the field to a gate on to a road by the front door of Springbank Cottage. Descend the surfaced track to enter a farmyard and continue left over a stone stile. Go over the hill, following the path that is parallel to the wall and then take the stile into a narrow ginnel. Follow this down, with a high garden wall to the right, round the corner and descend to a junction of roads. Go left on a private road/public footpath, and then bear right at the fork. At the next junction turn right to descend the track and at the following junction go left down Charney Well Lane. When you get to another junction, turn left below the woods of Eden Mount to a junction with Hampsfell Road near the bottom of the hill and turn right. At the junction with a larger road go left (toilets to the right) and pass the church before descending to pass the clock tower and junction with the main road (B5277). Go left and then right to the car park.

Across Heughscar Hill's Roman Road

This walk leads to views over the second largest lake in the region, crosses a Roman road and takes in artefacts of prehistory.

DISTANCE 4.5 miles (7.2km)   MINIMUM TIME 2hrs

ASCENT/GRADIENT 740ft (225m) ▲▲▲   LEVEL OF DIFFICULTY +++

PATHS Surfaced roads, stony tracks, grassy tracks and hillside

LANDSCAPE Village, dale and open fell

SUGGESTED MAP OS Explorer OL5 The English Lakes (NE)

START / FINISH Grid reference: NY 470244

DOG FRIENDLINESS Under strict control as sheep and ponies roam open fell

PARKING Pay car parks either side of bridge

PUBLIC TOILETS Pooley Bridge village centre

This is a relatively gentle and straightforward hill walk, traversing green turf, bracken and white limestone pavement. It offers extensive views west over Ullswater, north across the stone buildings of Pooley Bridge and east to the agricultural plains of the Eden Valley. Features of the walk include attractive Pooley Bridge, where a stone arched bridge crosses the River Eamont, crossing the High Street Roman road and an examination of the fascinating remains from prehistory found on Moor Divock.

Antiquities of Moor Divock

Ancient relics of prehistory, scattered across the high shoulder of Moor Divock, add an air of mystery and intrigue to this outing. Who were the bygone race of peoples who left their silent sentinels standing on this lonely windswept moor?

The short section of the High Street Roman road taken on this walk leads directly to the Cockpit stone circle and, although this isn't a circle of upright standing stones, it is quite distinct and unmistakable. Two concentric stone circles, some standing, some fallen, contain a stone and earth circular bank up to 3ft (1m) high. It has an internal radius of around 85ft (26m) and, as it is thought to be of Bronze Age origin, c2000 BC, it predates the Roman road. In more recent times, it was most probably used for cockfighting. This pastime, once popular in the Lake District, was outlawed in 1849.

Crouched Skeleton

Extending south east from here is desolate Moor Divock where, hidden amongst the stark landscape of coarse hill grass, bracken, heather and bog, are many prehistoric burial mounds and cairns. A raised mound known as White Raise, presumably because of the white quartz which marks its rocks, when partially excavated in the 19th century revealed a crouched skeleton in one of its cists (a coffin or burial chamber of stone or wood). Near by, the Cop Stone, a knarled standing stone some 5ft (1.6m) high, tops a low hill and provides a direction indicator in this otherwise rather featureless landscape. Local sports were held by this stone up until 1800 and tradition claims that an avenue of standing stones known as the Shap Avenue once led to it. Near by, two further Bronze Age stone circles referred to as Moor Divock 4 and Moor Divock 5, have been partially excavated to reveal urns and ashes.

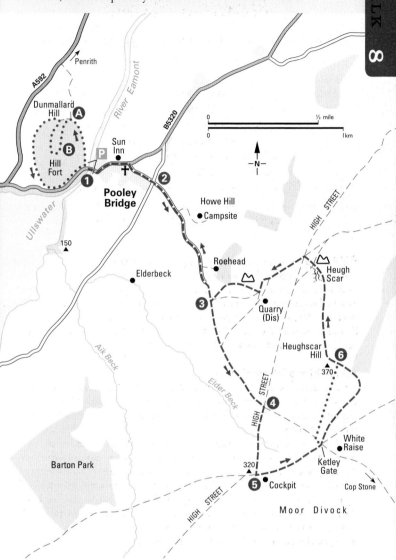

WALK 8 DIRECTIONS

❶ From the bridge crossing the River Eamont follow the main street (B5320) through the centre of Pooley Bridge. Walk on past the church then turn right to follow the pavement along Howtown Road.

❷ At the junction continue over the crossroads. The road rises and becomes pleasantly tree-lined before ending at an unsurfaced track beneath Roehead. A pair of gates lead on to the open moor.

❸ Go through one of the gates and climb the wide track,

continuing to where the going levels and the track crosses the High Street Roman road.

4 Bear right along the resurfaced stretch of Roman road to reach a low circular ancient wall of earth and stone. This, the Cockpit, is the largest of the prehistoric antiquities on Moor Divock.

WHERE TO EAT AND DRINK

There are numerous cafés and inns catering for a wide range of tastes in the village of Pooley Bridge. Particularly notable is the Sun, an unspoiled 18th-century coaching inn, with extensive oak beams, panelling and open fires. It offers excellent bar meals and a fine range of real ales brewed at the local Jennings Brewery in Cockermouth.

5 A way leads back diagonally north by the shallow shake holes (sinkholes) to the original track at Ketley Gate. (A little to the right, White Raise burial cairn is worthy of attention.) Either follow the track (the route marked on the map), which leads off north-east ascending to a walled wood high

WHAT TO LOOK OUT FOR

The High Street Roman road is followed for a short section of this walk. In its full length, the road traverses the high eastern Lakeland fells exceeding an altitude of 2,500ft (762m) in several places. It stretches from the Troutbeck Valley near Ambleside to Brougham by the River Eamont, where it intercepts the main south-east/north-west Roman arterial road. Today, whilst it may seem a rather wet and boggy affair, a problem made worse by the frequent passage of horses and mountain bikes, it remains a remarkable testament to the ambition of Roman engineering.

WHILE YOU'RE THERE

Just beyond Pooley Bridge, the shores of Ullswater, the region's second largest lake some 7.5 miles (12km) long, are a fine place to contemplate the beauty of the Lake District. Two beautifully preserved 19th-century boats, *Lady of the Lake* and *Raven*, run regular trips from the jetty stopping at the landing stages at Howtown and Glenridding.

on the hillside and then bear left to find the top of Heughscar Hill, or go left up a well-worn path through the bracken, starting by the stone parish boundary marker. The flat summit of the hill occupies a commanding position offering rewarding views.

6 Proceed north along the high shoulder to pass the broken little limestone crag of Heugh Scar below to the left. At the end of the scar make a steep descent of the grassy hillside crossing a track and continuing down to the point where another track and the grassy lane of the High Street Roman road cross each other. Descend to the left taking the track which passes below the Roman road and head in the general direction of Ullswater. Note a lime kiln and little quarry to the left. Continue the descent to the corner of a stone wall marked by a large sycamore tree. Follow the route which falls steeply down beside the stone wall. Bear left near the bottom of the incline and gain the original broad track just above the gates near Roehead. Return by the same road back to Pooley Bridge.

Dunmallard Hill Fort

Steep tree-clad slopes lead to a once important hill-fort.
See map and information panel for Walk 8

WALK 9

DISTANCE *1.5 miles (2.4km)* MINIMUM TIME *1hr*

ASCENT/GRADIENT *305ft (93m)* ▲▲▲ LEVEL OF DIFFICULTY ✦✦✦

WALK 9 DIRECTIONS
(Walk 8 option)

Although the name given on the map to the steeply wooded hill rising directly above Pooley Bridge is Dunmallard, it is known locally as Dunmallet. This is a striking defensive site, which looks directly down on the river crossing at Pooley Bridge. Unseen from below, and now lost in a thick canopy of trees, the top is adorned by the earthworks of a hill-fort dating from the Iron Age.

Two thousand years ago, Dunmallard lay within the territory of the Brigantes, a loose confederation of Celtic tribes whose influence extended from the Humber Estuary, north to the rivers Forth and Clyde. In those days a hill-fort was the ultimate symbol of local power, staking claim to the land around it, and acting as a refuge in time of war.

Leave the village at Point ❶ and cross the bridge. Go right towards the riverside car park, locating a kissing gate on the far side of its entrance, leading into the woods. Bear right and follow the ascending path.

At Point ❹, where a public footpath signed 'Dacre' cuts off down to the right, a worn muddy path climbs the bank to the left.

A few wooden steps mark the start of the ascent. This path leads steeply up the wooded slopes of Dunmallard before levelling to cross what was once a ditch surrounding the fort. A final section of steep bank leads over the earth ramparts of the fort and on to the tree-clad summit (Point ❸). Gaps in the foliage show how impressive a viewpoint this would be if the trees were thinned.

Traverse the plateau to its southern rim directly overlooking Ullswater, which is barely discernable through the trees, where a steep descent of 25ft (8m) leads to a track/ditch. (Take care here, if you think this descent is too difficult then retrace the route on the original path returning to Point ❹.) After the initial descent, bear right and follow the track (fallen trees will probably hinder your progress a little) going clockwise down the hill. Join the footpath just beyond Point A and go left in an anticlockwise direction downhill. Descend to a point just above the main road (B5320). Return to the car park, turn left at the road and recross the bridge back in to Pooley Bridge village.

Overleaf: Reflections on Ullswater (Walk 8)

High Arnside Knott

*This tree-clad knoll offers astonishing views
and a special ambiance.*

DISTANCE *5.5 miles (8.8km)*   MINIMUM TIME *3hrs*

ASCENT/GRADIENT *560ft (170m)* ▲▲▲   LEVEL OF DIFFICULTY ✦✦✦

PATHS *Foreshore, paths, some surfaced road, 2 stiles*

LANDSCAPE *Estuary and foreshore, mixed woods, limestone knoll*

SUGGESTED MAP *OS Explorer OL7 The English Lakes (SE)*

START / FINISH *Grid reference: SD 454786*

DOG FRIENDLINESS *Generally a good walk for energetic dogs*

PARKING *Free parking along promenade*

PUBLIC TOILETS *Above road located centrally along Arnside's seafront*

NOTE *Parts of foreshore impassable at high tide, beware of rapidly incoming
tides and quicksand; some unguarded little crags*

WALK 10 DIRECTIONS

Rising from the Kent Estuary to form a defiant outpost of resilient limestone, the heights of Arnside Knott are deservedly classed as an Area of Outstanding Natural Beauty. Bedecked with magnificent oak and mixed woods, rocky scree, hummocky grass, scattered bushes and the airy delights of steep open hillside, they also have the salty tang of the Kent Estuary which floods out into Morecambe Bay. Above the trees, to the north, the panoramic view of the high fells of Lakeland is nothing short of spectacular.

The little town of Arnside, with its station, viaduct crossing the estuary and elegant white limestone buildings, exudes a quiet feeling of Victorian affluence. Local children used to be thrilled by the tales of 'treading for fluke', literally fishing for the flatfish of that name, using your feet to hold them in place before scooping them out with your hands, and the terrors of the Arnside Bore. The former has been replaced by lines of conventional anglers equipped with modern tackle. The latter, a wave which runs in at the front of a rising tide, still presents a dramatic sight plus great danger out on the sands here, as the tide floods in at a gallop. A warning siren is sounded at the start of an incoming tide – heed its call.

WHERE TO EAT AND DRINK

Ye Olde Fighting Cocks, a traditional inn whose name tells its own tale about the history of the region, is situated centrally on the seafront and offers bar meals and real ales. Also on the front, near the end of the walk, is the Bay View Bakery and Café.

Walk along the promenade until, at the end of the surfaced road, by the entrance to Ashmeadow House, a walkway to the right continues above the sands. Continue along the path until it joins the foreshore. Continuing beneath Grubbins Wood, the path crosses mud, pebbles and a polished limestone outcrop, before it rounds a little headland to join a track. Depending on the tide, it may seem attractive to walk along the sands on the foreshore. This isn't recommended as quicksands are prevalent here and are undetectable until you sink. Bear right to New Barns. Leave the track and pass the buildings on the right following the foreshore, signed 'Public footpath subject to tides'. Round Frith Wood, following the path beneath the trees, high on the pebble beach. Keep on to rocky Blackstone Point. If the tide is high it's possible to climb to the path above the little cliffs and continue along the edge of the wood. Round the point and enter the little bay to walk along its brilliant white pebbles. It is usual to ascend here to follow the path above the little edge along the fringe of the woods of Arnside Park.

Round Park Point and continue along the edge. At a junction with a ruined stone wall, a track leads steeply up to the left to join another track in the woods, signed 'Far Arnside, Silverdale'. Go right and continue, to join a road and a caravan site. Go left along a high road and continue, to exit the site. Go along the road until a squeeze stile and gate lead through the wall on the left, signed 'Public footpath Arnside via The Knott'. Cross the fields to Hollins Farm and exit a stile gate on to a lane.

Go left through another gate and bear right following the path up the hillside of Heathwaite. A gate leads through the wall and out on to a track in the woods. Go straight across and ascend the stony track, continuing up into Arnside Knott Wood. At a fork bear left to a little gate then turn right, climbing steeply to a toposcope. Follow the path beyond this, back into the wood and turn left at a junction. Continue up to a bench near the summit. A path rising to the right leads to the trig point.

Go left, descend the path to a gate leading through the wall and continue down the field of Red Hills. Bear right to the bottom right corner of the field where a gate enters the woods. Descend the track through the woods to emerge on a road. Keep left until a road bears sharp right to descend to a larger road. Go right along this for a short way to join the Silverdale road. Bear left down to the seafront.

WALK 11

Along Ullswater's Shore to Silver Point

From the shores of Ullswater to one of its most spectacular viewpoints.

DISTANCE 4 miles (6.4km)   **MINIMUM TIME** 1hr 30min

ASCENT/GRADIENT 490ft (150m) ▲▲▲   **LEVEL OF DIFFICULTY** ✦✦✦

PATHS Stony tracks and paths, no stiles

LANDSCAPE Lake and fell views, mixed woodland

SUGGESTED MAP OS Explorer OL5 The English Lakes (NE)

START / FINISH Grid reference: NY 396159

DOG FRIENDLINESS Passes through working farm and open hillside grazed by sheep, dogs must be under control at all times

PARKING Pay-and-display car park opposite Patterdale Hotel

PUBLIC TOILETS Opposite White Lion in Patterdale village centre

---

The elongated hamlet of Patterdale has a rugged, mountain quality. Sited below the mighty Helvellyn massif its straggle of houses, inn, hotel, mountain rescue base, church and school have a bleakness about them. A perfect contrast to the splendour of Ullswater, whose southern shore lies hardly a stone's throw away. This walk strolls through mixed woodland and open aspect above the shores of the lake to visit the famed viewpoint of Silver Point. The adventurous may wish to make the scramble to the top of Silver Crag, as did horsedrawn coach parties of old, for a better view of the lake.

Ullswater

Undoubtedly one of the loveliest of the lakes, the three legs of Ullswater add up to a total length of 7.5 miles (12.1km) with an average width of 0.5 mile (800m) and a maximum depth of 205ft (62.5m). It is Lakeland's second largest lake, not quite measuring up to Windermere. Its waters are exceptionally clear and in the deepest part of the lake, off Howtown, lives a curious fish called the schelly; a creature akin to a freshwater herring.

Apart from rescue and Park Ranger launches, you won't see many power boats here, but Ullswater 'Steamers' have three boats operating between Glenridding and Pooley Bridge during the summer. Alfred Wainwright (1907–91), known for his seven *Pictorial Guides to the Lakeland Fells*, regarded this to be a part of one of the most beautiful walks in the Lakes. Preservation of the lake in its present form is due to a concerted campaign, led in Parliament by Lord Birkett, against the proposed Manchester Corporation Water Act in 1965. Although the act was passed, and water is extracted from the lake, the workings are hidden underground and designed in such a way as to make it impossible to lower the water level beyond the agreed limit.

Among the trees, beside the shore, it was the golden yellow daffodils of this lake that inspired William Wordsworth's most widely known poem, *I wandered lonely as a cloud* or *Daffodils* as it often referred to (published in 1807). His sister Dorothy recorded the event vividly in her diary: 'I never saw daffodils so beautiful. They grew among the mossy stones about and around them, some rested their heads upon these stones as on a pillar for weariness and the rest tossed and reeled and danced and seemed as if they verily laughed with the wind that blew them over the lake.' There is no doubt that this later helped William to pen his famous verse.

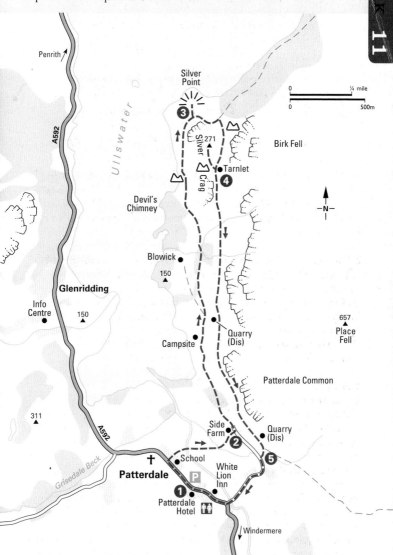

WALK 11 DIRECTIONS

❶ From the car park walk to the road and turn right towards the shore of Ullswater. Pass the school to a track leading off right, through the buildings. Follow the unsurfaced track over a bridge and continue through the buildings of Side Farm to join another unsurfaced track.

❷ Turn left along the undulating track, with a stone wall to the left, and pass through mixed woodland, predominantly oak and ash, before open fellside appears above. Proceed along the path above the campsite and pass a stand of larch before descending to cross a little stream above the buildings of Blowick, seen through the trees below. The path ascends again to crest a craggy knoll above the woods of Devil's Chimney. Make a steep descent following the path through the rocks before it levels to traverse beneath the craggy heights of Silver Crag. A slight ascent, passing some fine holly trees, gains the shoulder of Silver Point and an outstanding view of Ullswater. A short there-and-back to the tip is worthwhile.

❸ Follow the path, which sweeps beneath the end of Silver Crag and continue to pass a small stream before a steep stony path, eroded in places, breaks off to the right. Ascend this, climbing diagonally right, through the juniper bushes. Gain the narrow gap which

separates Silver Crag to the right from the main hillside of Birk Fell to the left. This little valley is quite boggy and holds a small tarnlet.

❹ If you don't care for steep, exposed ground, follow the high narrow path to make a gradual descent south in the direction of Patterdale. But for those with a head for heights, a short steep scramble leads to the top of Silver Crag and a wonderful view. Care must be exercised for steep ground lies in all directions. Descend back to the ravine and the main path by the same route. The path is easy though it traverses the open fellside and may be boggy in places. Pass open quarry workings, where there is a large unfenced hole next to the path (take care), and continue on, to cross over the slate scree of a larger quarry. Bear right to descend by a stream and cross a little footbridge leading to the gate at the end of a track.

❺ Go left through the gate and follow the lane which leads through the meadows. Cross the bridge and join the road. Bear right through Patterdale to return to the car park.

Brant Fell Above Bowness-on-Windermere

The woods, open spaces and breathtaking views over Windermere contrast markedly with the bustle below.

DISTANCE 3.5 miles (5.7km)   **MINIMUM TIME** 1hr 15min

ASCENT/GRADIENT 525ft (160m) ▲▲▲   **LEVEL OF DIFFICULTY** ✦✦✦

PATHS Pavement, road, stony tracks, grassy paths, 2 stiles

LANDSCAPE Town, mixed woodland, open fell, lake and fell views

SUGGESTED MAP OS Explorer OL7 The English Lakes (SE)

START / FINISH Grid reference: SD 398966

DOG FRIENDLINESS Popular route for dogs; busy roads and sheep grazing, so must be under control

PARKING Fee car park on Glebe Road above Windermere lake

PUBLIC TOILETS At car park and above information centre

Walking from the honeypot of Bowness-on-Windermere on a busy summer weekend, it is hard to imagine that just above the lakeside bustle there is a world of quiet solitude and space. Well there is, and this walk takes you there. With relatively little effort you can crest the heights of Brant Fell and enjoy a wonderful view out over Windermere to the Coniston fells and the central heights of the Lake District up to the mighty Fairfield.

Bowness-on-Windermere

Fed by the high rainfall of the Lake District fells, via the rivers Brathay, Rothay and Troutbeck, Windermere is England's largest natural lake. It stretches some 12 miles (19km) in length, is up to 1 mile (1.6km) wide in places, and reaches a depth of 220ft (67m). The Romans built their fort of Galava at Waterhead, on the northern tip of the lake.

Overlooked by this walk, the privately owned Belle Isle is said to have been used since Roman times. Today, this island is supplied by a little boat, which serves the 38 acre (15ha) estate. Belle Isle's interesting circular house, restored after extensive fire damage in 1996, was originally erected by Mr English in 1774. Apparently William Wordsworth accredited Mr English with the honour of being the first man to settle in the Lake District for the sake of the scenery. There have been many more since.

The main gateway and access point to the lake, Bowness-on-Windermere is today the most popular holiday destination in the Lake District. Over 10,000 boats for recreation are registered on the lake. Once the Oxenholme and Kendal-to-Windermere railway line opened in 1847 the town developed rapidly. Windermere town grew around the station from the nucleus of what was once a small village; it was the railway company that named the station Windermere to attract a trade, although it is some distance from the lake.

In the late 19th century wealthy businessmen, principally from industrial towns in Lancashire, built luxurious residences overlooking the lake. Many of these private houses are now hotels, such as the Langdale Chase, whilst Brockhole has been the National Park Visitor Centre since the late 1960s.

BOWNESS-ON-WINDERMERE

The Belsfield Hotel overlooking Bowness Bay was bought in 1860 by Henry Schneider, the chairman of the prosperous Barrow Steelworks and Shipworks. Reputedly he left his luxurious home and boarded his steam yacht SL *Esperance*, where he breakfasted travelling across the lake to Lakeside. He then journeyed by steam train, he owned the railway and had his own private carriage, to the works in Barrow.

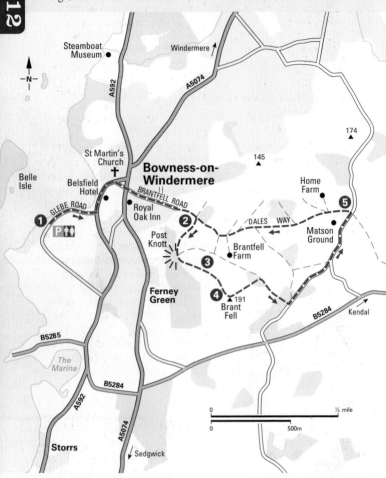

WALK 12 DIRECTIONS

❶ Take Glebe Road into Bowness town. Swing left and, opposite the steamer pier, go right over the main Windermere road and then turn left. Opposite the impressive Church of St Martin turn right to ascend the little street of St Martins Hill. Cross the Kendal road to climb Brantfell Road directly above. At the head of the road a little iron gate leads on to the Dales Way, a grassy and stony path which climbs directly up the hillside. Continue to a kissing gate by the wood, leading on to a lane.

❷ Pass through the kissing gate and turn right, signposted 'Post Knott', to follow the stony lane. Continue on the lane rising through the woods until it crests a height near the flat circular top

BOWNESS-ON-WINDERMERE

of Post Knott. Bear left and make the short ascent to the summit. The view from here was once exceptional but is now obscured by trees. Retrace a few steps back to the track then bear right to find a kissing gate leading out of the wood on to the open hillside.

3 Beyond the kissing gate take the grassy path, rising to a rocky shoulder. Cross the shoulder and first descend, then ascend to a ladder stile in the top corner of the field by some fir trees. Cross the stile then bear right to ascend directly up the open grassy flanks of Brant Fell to its rocky summit.

4 Go left (north-east) from the top of the fell, following a line of cairns down to a kissing gate. Descend through a young plantation to a second gate and a track. Turn right and follow the track to a stile and gate leading out to a road. Turn left along the road and continue left at the junction, to pass Matson Ground. Immediately beyond is a kissing gate on the left, waymarked for the Dales Way.

5 Go through the kissing gate and continue down the path to cross a track and pass through a kissing gate into another field. Keep along the track beneath the trees and beside a new pond, until the path swings left to emerge through a kissing gate on to a surfaced drive. Go right along the drive for 30yds (27m) until the path veers off left through the trees to follow the fence. An iron gate leads into a field. Follow the grassy path, first descending and then rising to an iron gate in the corner of the field. Continue to join a grassy track and go through the kissing gate. Cross the surfaced drive of Brantfell Farm and keep straight on to another kissing gate leading into a field. Follow the path, parallel to the wall, descending the hill to intercept a track, via a kissing gate, and regain Point **2**. Retrace your steps back to Glebe Road.

WALK 13

Lilies and Lakes Seen from Loughrigg

Above little Ambleside, Loughrigg Fell looks out to lake, dale and high fell.

DISTANCE 3.25 miles (5.2km)   MINIMUM TIME 1hr 45min

ASCENT/GRADIENT 575ft (175m) ▲▲▲   LEVEL OF DIFFICULTY ✦✦✦

PATHS Road, paths and tracks, can be muddy in places, 3 stiles

LANDSCAPE Town, park and open hillside with views to high fells

SUGGESTED MAP OS Explorer OL7 The English Lakes (SE)

START / FINISH Grid reference: NY 375047

DOG FRIENDLINESS Under control; busy roads, park, sheep grazing

PARKING Ambleside central car park

PUBLIC TOILETS At car park

The favourite of many, Loughrigg is a delightful low fell, which runs from Ambleside and the head of Windermere lake towards both Langdale and Grasmere. This circuit walk crosses the River Rothay by Miller Bridge and rises to a craggy viewpoint before traversing the small Lily Tarn to return via the stone lane of Miller Brow.

With the exception of possibly thick mist or cloud, this is a walk for all seasons and most weather conditions. The views, south over Waterhead and down Windermere and north over the wooded vale of Rydal into the high mountain drama of the Fairfield Horseshoe, are some of the most evocative in the region. The delightful detail of tree, rocky knoll, heather, bracken and the white and green cup and saucers of the lilies on Lily Tarn, contrast with the grand open views of mountain, dale and lake.

Ambleside

Even before the heights of lovely Loughrigg are reached, the varied slate stone buildings of Ambleside provide an intriguing start to the walk. Indeed, despite recent developments, there is a lot more to this little town than just being the outdoor equipment capital of Britain. Sited in the old county of Westmorland, Ambleside has long been a site of occupation. Bronze Age remains, c2000 BC can be seen on the nearby fells and the Galava Roman fort, near Waterhead, was one of the most important in north-west England.

How Head, just up the Kirkstone road, one of the oldest surviving buildings in old Ambleside, is located in the area known as Above Stock. Sections of this fine stone house date back to the 16th century and it was once the lodge of the Master Forester of the Barony of Kendal. It has massive circular chimneys, a typical Westmorland feature, stone mullioned windows and incorporates stone from the old Roman fort at Waterhead and cobbles from the bed of Stock Ghyll Beck.

Stock Ghyll once served as the heartbeat of the town when, some 150 years ago, it provided water power for 12 watermills. On this walk we pass a restored waterwheel, immediately followed by the famous Bridge House, one of the most photographed buildings in the Lake District. Spanning the beck, this tiny 17th-century building is said to have been built thus to avoid paying land tax. Locally

it is said to have once housed a family with six children. It is n
information centre for the National Trust. Ambleside has become a
resort with shops, hotels and restaurants, and is a convenient base fo
the rest of the Lake District.

Ambleside

Golden Rule Inn

Daisy's Café

Windermere

Museum

Bridge House

Waterhead

Windermere

Rothay Park

Galava Roman Fort

A5075

A591

Miller Bridge

Rydal

River Rothay

Brow Head Farm

Clappersgate

Lily Tarn

Old Clubhouse

Loughrigg Fell

R Brathay

A593

B5286

224

246

B

A

Scartufts

Black Mire

289

0   ½ mile

0   500m

335

Loughrigg Tarn

Coniston

N

WALK 13 DIRECTIONS

❶ Take the wooden footbridge from the car park and go right, along the Rydal road to pass the waterwheel and Bridge House. At the junction bear right along Compston Road. Continue to the

next junction, with the cinema on the corner, then bear right to cross the side road and enter Vicarage Road alongside the chip shop. Pass the school and enter Rothay Park. Follow the main path through the park to emerge by a flat bridge over Stock Ghyll

... Cross this then go left to cross over the stone arched Miller Bridge spanning the River Rothay.

2 Bear right along the road over the cattle grid until, in a few paces, a steep surfaced road rises to the left. Climb the road, which becomes unsurfaced, by the buildings of Brow Head Farm. At the S-bend beyond the buildings, a stone stile leads up and off left. Pass through the trees to find, in a few dozen paces, a stone squeeze stile. Pass through this, cross a little bridge and climb the open hillside above. The paths are well worn and a variety of routes are possible. For the best views over Windermere keep diagonally left. Rising steeply at first, the path levels before rising again to ascend the first rocky knoll. Cross a stile and a higher, larger knoll offering definitive views of the Fairfield Horseshoe to the north and over Windermere to the south.

3 Beyond this, the way descends to the right, dropping to a well-defined path. Follow the path to pass a little pond before cresting a rise and falling to lovely little Lily Tarn (flowers bloom late June to September). The path skirts the right edge of the tarn, roughly

following the crest of Loughrigg Fell before joining a wall on the left. Follow this down through a kissing gate and the base of a further knoll. This is ascended to another worthy viewpoint.

4 Take the path descending right to a prominent track below. Bear right to a gate which leads through the stone wall boundary of the open fell and into a field. Continue to descend the track, passing an interesting building on the left, the old golf clubhouse. Intercept the original route just above the buildings of Brow Head.

5 Continue to cross Miller Bridge then, before the flat bridge, bear left to follow the track by the side of Stock Ghyll Beck. Beyond the meadows a lane through the houses leads to the main Rydal road. Bear right on the road to the car park beyond the fire station.

To Loughrigg Fell Top

*A circumnavigation of the shoulder of Loughrigg
provides wonderful views.*
See map and information panel for Walk 13

DISTANCE *5 miles (8km)*   MINIMUM TIME *2hrs 30min*

ASCENT/GRADIENT *690ft (210m)* ▲▲▲   LEVEL OF DIFFICULTY ✦✦✦

WALK 14 DIRECTIONS
(Walk 13 option)

At Point **Ⓐ** bear left and descend into a boggy hollow. Cross the stream and bear right to find the main, largest and most distinct path. Other paths climb more directly above this point and tend to be a little more strenuous. The main path bears right, over Black Mire, before curving left to ascend the hillside. Climb steeply to gain a col. Steep craggy outcrops lie to the right. Beyond the col, the path levels and the going eases. Swing slightly left, to round a little tarnlet, then head for a shallow natural corridor, which ascends the high shoulder. Bear left at the head of the slope up steep steps to find the summit of Loughrigg Fell in a few hundred paces. A large cairn and stone trig point stand above the bracken, heather, tarnlets and outcrops.

Even the most discerning hill walker cannot fail to be impressed by the view from Loughrigg Fell. It is staggeringly good, both in terms of distance and in content. From here the high fells of the region, Coniston Old Man, Wetherlam, the Scafells, Bowfell, the Langdale Pikes, Dollywagon Pike, Fairfield and Red Screes, contrast dramatically with the woods, lakes and dales spread below. Those wishing to see the full extent of Grasmere lake may wish to continue walking a little further along the felltop here before returning to the summit.

From the summit return to the top of the shallow corridor taken in the ascent then follow the path that swings away to the left (roughly north-east). Pass a little tarnlet before descending by the stream, following another little natural corridor. Bear right and cross the stream just before the going steepens. An easy descent follows and leads towards a flat and rather boggy area known as Scartufts. Swing left before a little tarnlet and circumnavigate a rocky bracken-covered knoll. Beyond the knoll go right at the junction of paths to take the path heading south. Follow the little footpath over the flat boggy ground to pass another knoll. The path bears slightly left and traverses the left edge of Black Mire. The driest alternative from here is to keep left to join a large, distinct stony footpath at the corner of a dry-stone wall. Continue in the same direction following the line of the wall to intercept a track and a gate in the wall. Join the original route of Walk 13 at Point **Ⓑ**.

Waterfalls of Aira Force (Walk 15)

Hairy Aira Force

Ascend and descend the river gorge of Aira and High Force beneath the hamlet of Dockray.

DISTANCE 3 miles (4.8km) MINIMUM TIME 2hrs
ASCENT/GRADIENT 460ft (140m) ▲▲▲ LEVEL OF DIFFICULTY ✦✦✦
PATHS Stony tracks, steps, grassy paths and surfaced road
LANDSCAPE Pinetum, tree-lined river gorge, woods and open meadow
SUGGESTED MAP OS Explorer OL5 The English Lakes (NE)
START / FINISH Grid reference: NY 400200
DOG FRIENDLINESS Under very good control; narrow paths with steep drops, sheep pastures and open road
PARKING National Trust pay-and-display car park beneath falls
PUBLIC TOILETS At car park

WALK 15 DIRECTIONS

This circular walk climbs the tree-clad gorge of Aira Beck to pass two waterfalls, before continuing to ascend through meadows and natural woodland to the hamlet of Dockray. The lower, larger waterfall, Aira Force, is the more famous of the two. It offers an impressive sight from the viewpoint stone bridges above and below the falls. The beck cascades some 70ft (21m) vertically down a narrow rocky chasm into the pool beneath the lower bridge.

WHAT TO LOOK OUT FOR

A short distance from the entrance to the car park, occupying a commanding position on the hillside of Gowbarrow Fell and overlooking Ullswater, stand the impressive castle-like walls of Lyulph's Tower. Although the façade of the building is a rather grand folly, the structure it incorporates is still a working farm. The building was originally a pele tower modified by Charles Howard of Greystoke around 1780.

Particularly when in spate, the upper falls of High Force, which fall some 35ft (11m), are also impressive. Broader than Aira Force the falls resemble the rapids of an American river canyon. View them from the east bank, when ascending, from the outcropping bed of waterworn rocks above. Care must be taken, particularly when it's wet, as the rocks can be very slippery and there are no safeguards to prevent a fall.

While the waterfalls are a major attraction, the whole area surrounding the beck is a delightful mix of pine and exotic trees. It was purchased by the National Trust when the estate of Gowbarrow Park came up for sale in 1906. It had been owned by the Howard family of Greystoke Castle, who landscaped the area around the force. In 1846 they created a pinetum and pleasure garden, planting over half a million native and ornamental trees and establishing a network of tracks, footpaths and bridges. They planted more than 200 specimen conifers, including firs, pines, spruces and cedars from all over the world including a Sitka spruce from North America which now stands at around 120ft (37m) high.

Leave the car park beneath the arch, and cross the field until the path leads right into the woods. Go right, over the footbridge, to cross Aira Beck and continue following the terraced track up its east side. Take the low route to gain the impressive view of Aira Force from the bottom bridge, before climbing to the upper narrow stone arched bridge via the steps and hand rails. The view directly down the chasm and waterfall from the upper bridge is quite breathtaking and not for those averse to heights.

WHERE TO EAT AND DRINK

The Aira Force Café can be found in the car park and on a sunny day the outside benches offer a pleasant place for a cuppa or light meal. The Royal Hotel is in Dockray at the half way point of the walk. This 16th-century coaching inn once served merchants travelling north and south across the Scottish border – a Scottish coat of arms lies above the door. Bar meals are served all year.

Continue to follow the path up the east bank (true left) of the beck. A short deviation may be made by taking a wooden bridge which leads left, off the main path, to cross over a ravine to a viewpoint. Return to the main path and continue to the delightful rocky falls of High Force. (Alternatively you can greatly foreshorten the walk by returning to the car park down the opposite side of the beck from here.) There's a viewpoint from the rocky slabs above. In times of

spate it is probably safest to leave a close inspection until you return to High Force from the Dockray road to the west.

Keep along the narrow stony path above the beck. Go through a narrow wooden gate bearing a notice 'Farmland – keep dogs on the lead' to enter a small natural wood of hazel, silver birch, oak, ash, alder, rowan and sycamore. It seems light and airy compared with the thicker pinewoods found at the start of the walk. Beyond the wood, fields lead easily to a junction of ways. Go left and cross the beck via a bridge. Rise, to pass the buildings, and follow the track into Dockray and a junction with the road opposite the Royal Hotel.

Turn left down the road and continue until opposite the old quarry car park, where a path leads off left, signed 'Aira Force'. Pass through the kissing gate to leave the road and descend the field. The path then bears right above the west bank of the beck. At High Force it is possible to make a scrambled descent to the bank directly below the waterfall. This is a worthwhile viewpoint, though care should be taken. Follow the path above the beck to pass above the upper bridge of Aira Force. Continue the descent, following the path and steps along the edge of pine tress with open field to the right. This leads to a junction with the original path rising from the car park.

WHILE YOU'RE THERE

There are numerous little car parks and pull-ins off the A592 along the north-east shore of Ullswater. They all offer pleasant places from which to paddle, swim or contemplate this most beautiful lake.

A Haunting Experience on Souther Fell

Rolling grassy fells offer quiet solitude and an air of intrigue.

DISTANCE 6 miles (9.7km) MINIMUM TIME 3hrs

ASCENT/GRADIENT 985ft (300m) ▲▲▲ LEVEL OF DIFFICULTY +++

PATHS *Grassy and stony paths, open fellside, 4 stiles*

LANDSCAPE *Remote river valley, open exposed fellside*

SUGGESTED MAP *OS Explorer OL5 The English Lakes (NE)*

START / FINISH *Grid reference: NY 364300*

DOG FRIENDLINESS *Under control at all times; open fellside grazed by sheep*

PARKING *Wide verge above river in Mungrisdale*

PUBLIC TOILETS *None en route*

With an air of the theatrical, the little River Glenderamackin weaves a circuitous course around Souther Fell (pronounced sowter) passing through, on its meanderings, the little hamlet of Mungrisdale (pronounced mun-grize-dul). Whereas the central Lakeland fells are composed of hard volcanic rocks, Souther Fell and its neighbouring hills are made up of the relatively soft rocks of Skiddaw slate. The resultant smooth and rounded terrain of this mountain region gives an air of wild desolation. On this walk, a long gradual ascent following the river, provides an easy way to climb Souther Fell. The reward, once the heights are crested, are expansive views east over the plains of the Eden Valley and behind to the dark crags and combes of Bannerdale Fell and the great Blencathra mountain.

The majority of place-names in these parts are Celtic; Mungo (a Celtic missionary), Blencathra and Glenderamackin are typical examples. Indeed, the remains of an important Celtic hill-fort still forms a defensive ring around the nearby summit of Carrock Fell just to the north, and it is thought that northern Cumbria was still in the kingdom of Strathclyde in the 10th century. Perhaps originally associated with this ferocious tribe of Celts, locals have long said that a ghostly army of warriors marches over Souther Fell on Midsummer's Eve.

It all came to a head in 1745, the year the Jacobite Scot, Prince Charles Edward Stuart ('Bonnie' Prince Charlie) returned to march on England. Following reports that both soldiers and horsemen had been seen marching along the high shoulder of Souther Fell a group of 26 stationed themselves at a suitable vantage point in the valley below on the evening before midsummer, determined to lay low the rumours and speculation. To their incredulity they witnessed a rapidly moving line of troops, horses and carriages. The line spread right across the high summit shoulder of the fell in a continuous chain. Steep places and rocky outcrops neither slowed nor disrupted progress of this huge army. They couldn't believe their eyes yet only darkness put an effective end to these strange events. The next day there was nothing to be seen so, with considerable trepidation, half expecting that the invasion from over the border had begun, a party climbed to the summit, where they found nothing. Not a mark in the grass, no footprint, hoof-print or wheel rut, and of an army there was not the remotest sign.

SOUTHER FELL

So convinced were the 26 men, and determined that their integrity should be respected, that they all swore an oath before a magistrate as to what they had seen. It remains a mystery, yet Bonnie Prince Charlie was to invade in the November of that same year.

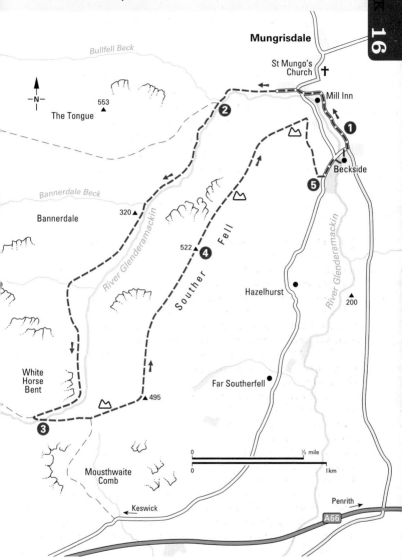

WALK 16 DIRECTIONS

❶ Head north up the road, following the River Glenderamackin upstream. Then bear right where the road crosses the stone bridge and continue to a hairpin bend. Go left to leave the road, pass the telephone kiosk, and follow the little lane between the cottages. Go through the gate and continue along the unsurfaced track above the north bank of the river. Now bear left and then cross little Bullfell Beck by a narrow footbridge.

2 Bear left off the steeply ascending track and follow a lesser stony track which traces a route along the right bank (true left) of the River Glenderamackin. The going is straightforward although the path has been eroded in places and there is a steep drop into the little river. Continue along the track, which is very boggy in places, to ford Bannerdale Beck. This is not difficult and it should be possible to keep dry by balancing on the stones. Round the shoulder of Bannerdale Fell; named White Horse Bent by the Ordnance Survey, should it be White Hawse Bent? Continue the ascent until a path falls left to a flat wooden footbridge to cross the River Glenderamackin, which is hardly 6ft (2m) wide at this point.

3 The path ascends the hillside striking diagonally left to climb to the top of the high grassy shoulder. Mousthwaite Comb lies down below to the right. Bear left, following the path and ascend the long shoulder of Souther Fell. You pass a large circular cairn of Skiddaw slate topped by a rock of white quartz and then continue along the level shoulder, heading north to a little rocky knoll – the summit.

4 Keep north and continue to descend the grassy nose of the fell. Easy at first, the angle steepens progressively until, nearing the base, the little craggy outcrops are best avoided by following the path to their left. The path is well

defined and soon leads to a stone wall near the bottom of the fell. At one time a little path led over a stile and directly down the field to the Mill Inn. Unfortunately this has now been blocked off and it is necessary to go right along by the wall, although this path is extremely boggy in places. Continue along by the wall until it bends left and a steep little descent leads to a surfaced road.

5 Go left down the road, through a gate until, at the bottom of the hill, a grassy lane continues on down to the River Glenderamackin, just upstream of the buildings of Beckside. Before reaching the ford that crosses the river, stone steps over the wall on the right give access to a narrow footbridge. Cross the bridge, and then go left to exit the field via a squeeze stile. Go right, climbing the grassy bank to the road. Head left and go upstream to return to the parking area.

St John's in the Vale

Exploring a compact valley and a wild fell.

DISTANCE *5 miles (8km)* MINIMUM TIME *2hrs 45min*

ASCENT/GRADIENT *1,115ft (340m)* ▲▲▲ LEVEL OF DIFFICULTY ✦✦✦

PATHS *Grassy paths and track, 8 stiles*

LANDSCAPE *Open fellside and river dale*

SUGGESTED MAP *OS Explorer OL5 The English Lakes (NE)*

START / FINISH *Grid reference: NY 318195*

DOG FRIENDLINESS *Under control at all times; open fellside grazed by sheep*

PARKING *Car park at Legburthwaite, head of St John's in the Vale*

PUBLIC TOILETS *At car park*

With St John's in the Vale to the east and the Naddle Valley extension of the Thirlmere Valley to the west, Naddle Fell forms an attractive little upland area which runs north from the end of the Thirlmere Reservoir towards the great northern fells of Blencathra and Skiddaw. Its three tops, Wren Crag, High Rigg and Naddle Fell itself, straddle a shoulder of craggy outcrops, sprinkled with a mix of bracken and ling heather. Tarnlets fill many of the hollows, rowan and Scots pine abound, and despite the presence of higher fells all around and roads in the dales below, this rugged fell has great charm and a surprising degree of anonymity.

This walk rises from Legburthwaite, at the head of the valley of St John's in the Vale, to traverse the length of the fell. Despite its higher neighbours it has a lovely sunny disposition and is a pleasant place to linger on a warm summer's day. Sunsets seen from here over Castlerigg stone circle and Keswick can be spectacular. The walk along the top offers unparalleled views of the great bastion of Castle Rock, and north to Skiddaw and Blencathra, before dropping to the hidden little Church of St John's in the Vale. Finally it returns along the vale itself.

The Chapel of St John's in the Vale

Entering through the little iron gate and archway of overhanging yew, the proportions of this slate roofed, low, narrow stone building, immediately seem just right. It's simple and unassuming like many other Lakeland country churches. With the parish history related on its assembled headstones it is a building in perfect harmony with its natural surroundings.

The quiet road which runs past was once of greater importance and linked communities on both sides of the high shoulder. Undoubtedly there has long been a church on this site and although the present building dates from 1845, as a plaque over the porch shows, headstones outside predate this considerably. It is thought that a reference in the chartulary of Fountain's Abbey to 'dommus sancti Johannis' – a house of St John – may refer to a church on this site in the 13th century. Otherwise the earliest definite reference to St John's is in 1554. The sundial is inscribed 'St John's Chapel, 1635' and a silver chalice (not kept within the church) was gifted in 1659. Although the chair in the sanctuary is dated 1865, the registers within the church date from 1776 onwards.

ST JOHN'S IN THE VALE

The church was once part of the parish of Crosthwaite, which stretched from the top of the hill just outside Keswick to the top of Dunmail Raise and included Thirlmere, Helvellyn and the stone circle at Castlerigg. With the flooding of Thirlmere Reservoir the parish is now somewhat diminished.

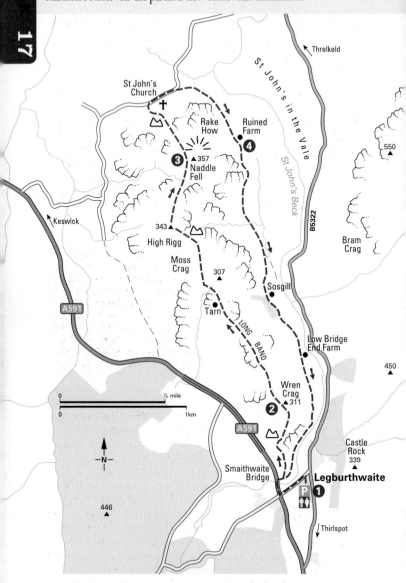

WALK 17 DIRECTIONS

1 Pass through the head of the car park to find a small gate leading on to the old road. Turn left and go down the lane to a gate that opens on to the verge of the busy A591. Turn right along this and cross Smaithwaite Bridge to a stile climbing the wall to the right. Cross the stile and take the path that rises to the left. This leads through a stand of magnificent Scots pine and climbs to the top of

ST JOHN'S IN THE VALE

Wren Crag with a view to Castle Rock on the opposite side of St John's in the Vale.

❷ Descend steeply into the dip and take the gap in the wall. Climb again to follow along above the rocky outcrops of Long Band. A grassy incline leads to a stile over the wire fence to the left. Cross this then follow it right, first rising then falling to pass a little tarn in a hollow. The route now descends to the left, dipping to reach a stile by a wall junction. Beyond the stile the path runs along the wall, climbing to pass through a corridor formed by the rocky knoll of Moss Crag. Immediately beyond the crag a boggy area forces you left. As you round it, turn left up the steep slope to the summit of High Rigg. A grassy ridge leads above the

shining tarns of Paper Moss to a hollow and pond. Ascend to the summit of Naddle Fell (sadly always unnamed on Ordnance Survey maps), the highest point of this walk which offers a superb view across to the high fells of Blencathra and Skiddaw.

❸ A wide path falls down the steepening hillside to the buildings by the road above St John's Church. Turn right down the road past the church to a gate and stile leading to a grassy track. Skirt the foot of the fell along this track. Below Rake How pass a ruined farm surrounded by sycamores and a giant overhanging yew.

❹ Keep along this track taking a high route right of and above Sosgill, to pass through three gates/stiles followed by a kissing gate into a larch and conifer plantation. Exit the trees via a kissing gate and continue to take the path to the right side of Low Bridge End Farm. Continue along the track through another series of gates and stiles to the point where the track meets the bank of St John's Beck, beneath Wren Crag. Here the track ends and a footpath continues above the river, rising through the trees to the grassy shoulder above the stile that leads back on to the A591. Turn left and left again to return to the car park and the start of the walk at Legburthwaite.

Coniston to Tarn Hows

Explore the delightful wooded intricacies of Yewdale before reaching the tourist favourite of Tarn Hows.

DISTANCE 6.75 miles (10.9km)   **MINIMUM TIME** 3hrs 30min

ASCENT/GRADIENT 885ft (270m) ▲▲▲   **LEVEL OF DIFFICULTY** ✦✦✦

PATHS Road, grassy paths and tracks, 4 stiles

LANDSCAPE Woods, field, fell, tarn and lake

SUGGESTED MAP OS Explorer OL7 The English Lakes (SE)

START / FINISH Grid reference: SD 303975

DOG FRIENDLINESS Fields grazed by sheep, reasonably suitable for dogs

PARKING Coniston car park by tourist information centre

PUBLIC TOILETS At car park

This long route of great variety, much interest and heart-stopping beauty contrasts the quiet mixed woods in and around the fringes of forgotten Yewdale, with the popular Tarn Hows. Rising from Coniston, quiet woods are interspersed with openness and tremendous views particularly when looking back over Coniston Water or to the mountains of Coniston Old Man and Wetherlam.

The waters of Tarn Hows represent the physical high point and, no matter how popular, cannot fail to seduce, before descent by Tom Gill leads to one of the most classic of all Lakeland farms, Yewdale Farm with its famous spinning gallery. A round of Yewdale follows with the row of yew trees in front of High Yewdale Farm commencing the return via Black Guards to Coniston. While there is quite a bit of ascent and descent the going could never be described as laborious.

Coniston Copper

Copper mining started in the bowels of the Coniston Old Man mountain in the Bronze Age. So extensive were these workings that when some German miners, brought over in Elizabethan times to kickstart 'modern mineral mining' in Britain, started work, they were shocked to find that the mountain was already riddled with workings. They referred to these earlier workings as 'the old men workings' which is possibly one derivation of the modern name Coniston Old Man.

Coniston Water is some 5 miles (8km) long and reaches a maximum depth of 184ft (56m). It is the third largest of the Lakeland lakes and once provided an important fish source for the monks of Furness Abbey. Many of their iron bloomery and charcoal burning sites remain intact around the shores of the lake. The copper mines were revitalised around 1859 and some 800 men worked in Coppermines Valley above the village. The railway was axed in the early 1960s and the village now relies principally on tourism.

Raised from the Lake

Speed ace Donald Campbell was killed on Coniston Water in 1967, attempting to beat his own water speed record of nearly 300mph (480kph). His boat, *Bluebird*, became airborne and crashed, but in 2001 it was raised from the bed of the lake. His body was also later recovered and was buried in St Andrew's Church.

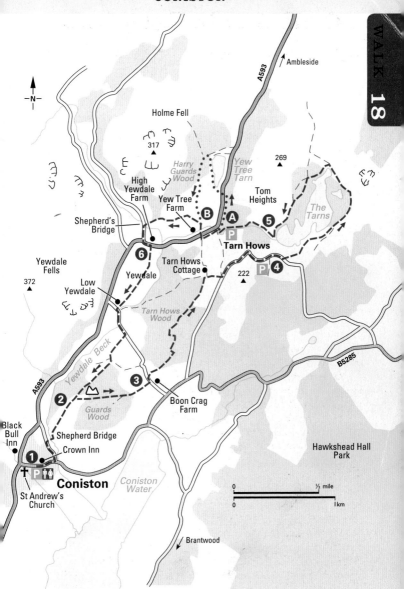

WALK 18 DIRECTIONS

1 Exit the car park on to the road (Tilberthwaite Avenue) and then turn right. Continue until, after a few hundred paces, a road leads off to the left. Follow this beyond the football field to Shepherd Bridge, which leads right over Yewdale Beck. Cross and then go immediately left over the low stone stile. The path leads above the river to a kissing gate and enters a field. Bear diagonally right towards the rocky outcrop and oak trees and then continue along to the right of a stone wall. In a little way the path leads directly to a recently renovated stone building.

W A L K 18

❷ Pass the building on the left. Ascend to pass through a gate. Fork right following the wall and then rise to a little gate through the stone wall that forms the perimeter of High Guards Wood. Climb steeply to the top of the hill through the Scots pine. Cross a ruined stone wall and follow the waymarked path to descend through Guards Wood. Exit the wood and continue down a stony track, muddy in places, to a gate and stile on to a stony lane.

❸ Go left up the lane. In a hundred paces go right through a gate. Rise with the grassy track until it swings right to pass through a gate/stile. The vague grassy track intercepts a fence with the larch plantation of Tarn Hows Wood below. Keep right along the track and continue to reach a steep, surfaced track. Tarn Hows Cottage is below to the left. Go right along the track to the Tarn Hows road. Go left, ascending the road and passing the car park, to find a track bearing off left above Tarn Hows.

❹ Follow the track to make an anticlockwise circumnavigation of the tarn. At the end is a little dam.

❺ Turn right at the dam and descend the path to the right of the beck. At the bottom go left across the footbridge then through Tom Gill car park to a gate on the far side. Follow the field-edge

path to another gate opposite Yew Tree Farm. Cross the road and go to the right of the farm, to a gate. Rise to pass through another gate, then go left above the fence. Keep along this track, around High Yewdale Farm, until a final gate leads on to the Hodge Close road. Turn left over Shepherd's Bridge and join the main Coniston road.

❻ Cross and go left until, opposite High Yewdale Farm, a path leads right along the line of yew trees. Pass the trees, and then go right, across the fields. At Low Yewdale farmyard go left along a lane, over a bridge, and continue to round a sharp bend. Go right ('Cumbria Way'), through the field. Beyond a stone wall the track ascends then bears right. Continue to enter Back Guards Plantation and follow the track through the wood. Pass through yew trees and descend to join the walk's outward route back into Coniston village and the car park.

To Yew Tree Tarn

Round a charming little tarn, traversing tall fir woods.
See map and information panel for Walk 18

DISTANCE *8 miles (12.9km)*   **MINIMUM TIME** *4hrs*
ASCENT/GRADIENT *885ft (270m)* ▲▲▲   **LEVEL OF DIFFICULTY** ✦✦✦

WALK 19 DIRECTIONS
(Walk 18 option)

At Point **Ⓐ** turn right to follow the signed little footpath leading above the Coniston road. The path is undulating, overhung by trees in many places and is in close proximity to the road. Soon you are forced down to road level. Cross over and then traverse the dam and footbridge on the far side, the outflow of Yew Tree Tarn.

The tarn was constructed for commercial trout fishing in the 1920s by the Marshall family, who owned the Monk Coniston estate – 'we stopped up the stream and made the lake itself'. It wasn't included in the 1930 deal between Beatrix Potter and the National Trust, and did not become Trust land until 1952. Since then they have managed and improved access to the shore, only recently rebuilding the dam with money from the Heritage Lottery Fund. The tarn is still a popular spot with local fly fishermen, who can be seen most days.

Follow the prominent path along the west shore. Go through a gate and continue, on a raised pathway briefly, to enter a stand of tall pine trees beyond the marshy head of the tarn. After 50yds (46m), break off left towards a gate in the wall on your left.

Pass through the gate and follow the path bearing left through Harry Guards Wood. Keep along to pass between two large boulders until, a little way further on, a gate leads left through the fence. Go through this and swing around the nose of the rise to find a natural corridor leading through the craggy outcrops (some boggy). Continue until the path becomes a grassy track and descends to Point **Ⓑ**, where you can rejoin Walk 18 back into Coniston.

WHAT TO LOOK OUT FOR

The recently refurbished stone building with mock twin towers below High Guards, Tarn Hows and Yew Tree Tarn have a common theme. They were all created by the Marshall family of Monk Coniston in the 19th century for sporting purposes. The building was built to house the Coniston foxhounds by James Garth Marshall in 1855. Tarn Hows, once three separate sheets of water, was dammed and stocked with fish. A similar fate befell the hay meadow now known as Yew Tree Tarn.

WALK 20

A Round of Rydal Water

*A circuit of Rydal Water via Loughrigg Terrace
and the Coffin Route.*

DISTANCE 3 miles (4.8km)   **MINIMUM TIME** 1hr 30min

ASCENT/GRADIENT 460ft (140m) ▲▲▲   **LEVEL OF DIFFICULTY** +++

PATHS Stony paths and tracks

LANDSCAPE Rydal Water nesting in wooded vale below high fells

SUGGESTED MAP OS Explorer OL7 The English Lakes (NE)

START / FINISH Grid reference: SD 348066

DOG FRIENDLINESS Generally suitable for dogs; grazing sheep,
2 road crossings

PARKING National Trust parking (fee), White Moss Common

PUBLIC TOILETS Below road at White Moss Common

WALK 20 DIRECTIONS

This classic walk of breathtaking beauty will surely be forever associated with the poet William Wordsworth (1770–1850). From all around the world people come here to see the landscape that so inspired him. His poetry broke with the conventional structure and stylised imagery of his day, to explore nature and human emotion in a new poetic language. He lived at Dove Cottage in Grasmere between 1799 and 1808 and at Rydal Mount from 1813 until his death in 1850.

WHILE YOU'RE THERE

Rydal church, partly designed by William Wordsworth, is a building worthy of closer inspection. Behind the church is Dora's Field, with its stand of oaks and pines, and full of golden daffodils between late March and early April. This piece of steeply dipping hillside beneath Rydal Mount, was dedicated by William Wordsworth to his daughter, Dora, who died at an early age.

Despite its popularity, this outing can never fail to inspire. Each season is different. Whether the lake is clad in ice, or the flora in springtime blossom, it is a landscape to lift the spirit. This walk, with a little ascent and descent, visits wood, lake and river. Dippers can often be seen on the river, swans on the lake, ravens on Nab Scar, and roe deer in the woods. The village of Rydal forms a convenient half-way point.

From the higher car park, walk above the road, cross the road and descend the steps which lead across the common to gain the track by the river. If you start in the car park below the road, beyond the low barrier, take the track into the wood. Proceed to cross a footbridge (toilets above to the right) and continue until the track nears the river. The two paths from both car parks lead to this point. Pass the bend in the river and continue along the track to bear left. Cross the footbridge over the river. Take the path slightly to the right straight on, through the woods away from the river. Ascend to a kissing gate leading to a stony track. Here, an alternative route bears left by the shoreline of Rydal Water.

Take the path above, which heads left to ascend through the bracken to a level path known as Loughrigg Terrace. Traverse left along the path to a fine viewpoint, overlooking the lake to Nab Cottage and Nab Scar. Continue along the path to round the next shoulder and cross a level area of slate waste. Beyond this, find the entrance to Rydal Cave, an old slate quarry. Descend the track directly below this and pass through a larch wood before the track bears right to pass a further quarry hole and caves. Keep along the track, which rounds a little bend before becoming a walled lane that descends between Jobson Close, below, and the woods of Rough Intake, above. Intercept a track and cross it, bearing left slightly, to find a path down to Rydal Water.

Bear right to enter woods by a gate. The path leads through the wood and then, with the lake just over to the left, walk through the field to intercept the River Rothay. Cross by the bridge on to the A591. The Badger Bar stands opposite. Bear right along the road until a lane leads uphill to the left.

Cross the road and follow the lane up to Rydal church and

WHAT TO LOOK OUT FOR

Rydal Mount was the last home of William Wordsworth. Open to the public, the house, with its family portraits, furniture and some of the poet's personal possessions, is set in exquisite gardens, designed by Wordsworth himself. Rented from Lady Diana le Fleming who lived in Rydal Hall, it was home to William, his wife and family and sister Dorothy.

Dora's Field, then steeper still to pass by Rydal Mount, the home of William Wordsworth. Immediately above Rydal Mount a track bears left. Pass through a gate and follow this track, the old Coffin Route which runs between Ambleside and Grasmere. Stony in places, the track is well defined, traversing clumps of oaks with a view south over Rydal Water. As the track rounds a bend and intercepts a wall there is a square stone on the right. This is the coffin rest stone, where the bearers once placed their burden for a break. There is a seat beyond this and then a gate leads through a wall and the track enters the woods above Nab Cottage.

Keep along the track and pass through a gate, to dip slightly, before making a short steep ascent. The wall above on the right at this point is an exposed part of the Thirlmere Aqueduct which runs all the way to Manchester. Round the shoulder and make a rocky descent to cross a stream. Keep on to a gate below a house above the track to the right. Through this gate a lane falls steeply down the hillside to the left. Take this lane through the wood to intercept the A591 just above the lower car park at White Moss Common.

Woods at Satterthwaite and Rusland

Follow paths, through forest and woodland, once trodden by charcoal burners, iron smelters and coppicers.

DISTANCE	4.75 miles (7.7km) MINIMUM TIME 2hrs
ASCENT/GRADIENT	1,017ft (310m) ▲▲▲ LEVEL OF DIFFICULTY ✦✦✦
PATHS	Mainly good paths and tracks throughout, 3 stiles
LANDSCAPE	Gentle hills cloaked in mixed woodland and forest
SUGGESTED MAP	OS Explorer OL7 The English Lakes (SE)
START / FINISH	Grid reference: SD 344912
DOG FRIENDLINESS	No special problems, take lead for roads and farmland
PARKING	Forest car park at Blind Lane
PUBLIC TOILETS	None on route; nearest at Grizedale Vsitor Centre

Although a serenely peaceful place today, it is not that long since the forest and the streams that course through it supported a range of industries, many of which had operated for centuries. Little more than 100 years ago, you would still have been able to find working watermills in the valleys and see woodcutters at work coppicing the trees. The air was once heavy with the smoke of charcoal burning or the acrid smell of iron smelting and the silence was disturbed by the dull thudding of forge hammers or the echoing screams of saws slicing timber into planks and spars. Strange as it may seem, if it had not been for that industrial tradition, the rich forests and woodlands that today lend so much character and beauty to this corner of Lakeland, might have disappeared long ago, replaced by the open sheep walks prevalent throughout so much of the countryside.

Medieval Industry

Before the Dissolution of the Monasteries, the monks at Furness Abbey managed extensive iron ore mines and needed a constant supply of charcoal to reduce it to iron. The woodland here provided a ready source of timber, but simply to fell the trees would have exhausted the stock before a new crop could be grown. However, by coppicing the boles a steady supply of small timber was guaranteed, since new wood could be harvested every 15 years or so. Bloomeries were established deep within the forest, for it was more economic to bring in the ore than take out the charcoal. After the monks were expelled, the estates passed into private hands and the industries continued to grow.

By the 18th century, new techniques needed power to drive machinery. Mills sprang up beside the streams, here powering bellows and forge hammers that beat impurities from the metal, which was being produced in ever-larger and more efficient furnaces around Backbarrow. This walk passes two former mills, Force Forge and Force Mills, as well as a reconstructed charcoal burner's hut in the forest beyond Satterthwaite.

Rich Habitat

Although the industry here has now disappeared, the forest remains an important resource, managed to provide a renewable supply of timber for today's

SATTERTHWAITE

manufacturers. It is also a rich wildlife habitat and valued as a recreational retreat by us humans. In many ways, the forest is being made to work just as hard today as it has ever done, and long may it remain for future generations to enjoy.

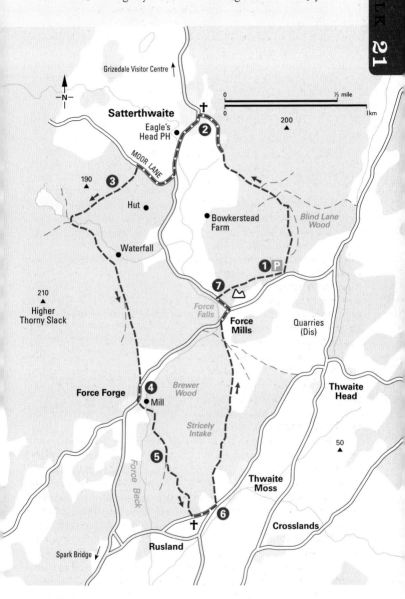

WALK 21 DIRECTIONS

❶ A path from the back of the car park, marked by green- and white-topped posts, heads right, over a rise to a forest trail. Walk left and, after 400yds (366m), turn left on to a path through birch wood. Go ahead over a junction at the top and descend to join a metalled track into the village of Satterthwaite.

WHILE YOU'RE THERE

Coppiced wood was used for a wide assortment of products, including barrels, baskets, hurdles and tanning bark. Another important industry was bobbin manufacturing, supplying the Pennine spinning and weaving sheds, which used them by the million. Nearby Stott Park Bobbin Mill operated from 1835 to 1971 and is now a working museum, where you can step back in time to see bobbins made just as they were in Queen Victoria's day.

2 Turn left by the church and walk through the village. After 0.25 mile (400m), at a left-hand bend, go right on to a track, Moor Lane, and then at a marker post, head left on to a rising path into the trees. Bear left at a post and shortly drop to a broader track.

3 Go right, over another hill and right again when you eventually reach a broad forest trail. Pass a waterfall and look out for bathers, part of the forest art project. Beyond, the track bends across the stream before rising to a junction. Turn left for 220yds (201m) and branch left again on to an unmarked, descending grass track.

WHAT TO LOOK OUT FOR

In a quiet corner behind Rusland's church lie the ashes of Arthur Ransome (1884–1967), loved by many for his wonderful stories of the *Swallows and Amazons*. He spent his childhood holidays at High Nibthwaite above Coniston and developed a lifelong passion for the area. Ransome worked for much of his life as a journalist, but came to live in the Lakes in 1925, where he wrote his famous children's books.

4 Emerging on to a lane at the bottom, go right, then turn in-between cottages at Force Forge. Through a gate on the right, go left by a tall beech hedge and across Force Beck. Continue through a deer fence along a winding path into Brewer Wood, bearing right when you shortly reach a crossing path.

5 After about 0.25 mile (400m), at a fork, bear left to a gap in the wall and carry on through trees. Reach an indistinct fork beyond the crest of the hill and take the right-hand branch, which descends to Rusland Reading Rooms. Cross out to the lane in front of the church and walk left.

WHERE TO EAT AND DRINK

Along the route, you'll pass the Eagle's Head at Satterthwaite, but even if you are not hungry at that stage, the home-cooked food is good enough to tempt you back at the end of the walk, it is only a short drive away. Alternatively, pop up to the tea rooms at Grizedale Visitor Centre, higher up the valley.

6 A little way along, leave the lane for a byway opposite a junction. Climb over the top of Stricely beside wooded pastures and eventually drop to a lane at Force Mills. Go right and then left to ascend beside Force Falls.

7 At a green and white post, part-way up the hill, turn right on to a path climbing steeply into a larch plantation. Keep right where the path forks, shortly passing through a gap in the wall. Go through another gap a few paces on and descend through the trees back to the car park.

Four Seasons by Elter Water and Loughrigg Tarn

Bluebell woods, a lake, a tarn, a waterfall and Little Loughrigg, make this a memorable outing.

DISTANCE *4 miles (6.4km)* **MINIMUM TIME** *2hrs*

ASCENT/GRADIENT *328ft (100m)* ▲▲▲ **LEVEL OF DIFFICULTY** +++

PATHS *Grassy and stony paths and tracks, surfaced lane, 4 stiles*

LANDSCAPE *Lake, tarn, fields, woods, open fellside, views to fells*

SUGGESTED MAP *OS Explorer OL7 The English Lakes (SE)*

START / FINISH *Grid reference: NY 328048*

DOG FRIENDLINESS *Under control at all time; fellside grazed by sheep*

PARKING *National Trust pay-and-display car park at Elterwater village*

PUBLIC TOILETS *Above car park in Elterwater village*

Although it does include steep sections of ascent and descent this is not a desperately difficult walk. There are outstanding views throughout its length. The little lake of Elter Water and the petite Loughrigg Tarn are among the prettiest stretches of water in the region. The former, really three interconnected basins, was originally named Eltermere, which translates directly from the Old Norse (Viking) into 'swan lake'. The swans are still here in abundance. Be careful they don't grab your sandwiches should you choose to eat your lunch sat on the wooden bench at the foot of the lake. The views over both lake and tarn, to the reclining lion profile of the Langdale Pikes, are particularly evocative.

Each season paints a different picture. Golden daffodils by Langdale Beck in early spring, bluebells in Rob Rash woods in May, yellow maple in Elterwater village in October and a thousand shades of green, everywhere, all summer. The river is dominant throughout the lower stages of the walk. It starts as the Great Langdale Beck, before emerging from the confines of Elter Water as the sedate River Brathay. Ascent then leads to the suspended bowl of Loughrigg Tarn, followed by the open fell freedom of Little Loughrigg. This is very much a walk for all seasons, and should the section through the meadows by the Brathay be flooded, then a simple detour can easily be made on to the road to bypass the problem.

Local Gunpowder Works

With all the quarrying and mining that once took place in the Lake District, including a little poaching for the pot, there used to be a considerable demand for 'black powder' or gunpowder. Elterwater Gunpowder Works, founded in 1824, once filled that demand. The natural water power of Langdale Beck was utilised to drive great grinding wheels or millstones. Prime quality charcoal came from the local coppices, whilst saltpetre and sulphur were imported. In the 1890s the works employed around 80 people. Accidental explosions did occur, notably in 1916 when four men were killed. The whole enterprise closed down in 1929. Today the site is occupied by the highly desirable Langdale Timeshare organisation, with only the massive mill wheels on display to bear witness to times past.

ELTER WATER

Of course, the raw ingredients had to be brought in and the highly explosive gunpowder taken away. That was done by horse and cart. Clydesdales were preferred for their huge strength and considerable intelligence. On workdays they would be harnessed up and on special occasions they had their mains plaited and ribboned and they were decorated with polished horse brasses. The horses have long gone but some of their brasses remain fixed to the oak beams in the Brittania Inn.

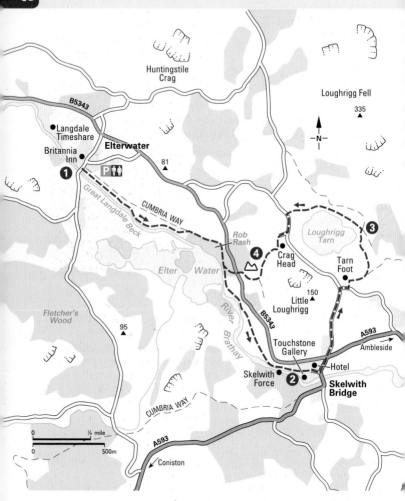

WALK 22 DIRECTIONS

❶ Pass through a small gate to walk downsteam above Great Langdale Beck. Continue to enter the mixed woods of Rob Rash. A little gate leads through the stone wal; the open foot of Elter Water lies to the right. Continue along the path through the meadows above the river. Note that this section can be wet and is prone to flooding. Pass through the gate and enter mixed woods. Keep along the path to pass Skelwith Force waterfall down to the right. A little bridge leads across a channel to a viewing point above

ELTER WATER

the falls. Keep along the path to pass through industrial buildings belonging to Kirkstone Quarry.

② Touchstone Gallery is on the right, as the path becomes a small surfaced road. Continue to intercept the A593 by the bridge over the river where there are picnic benches. Turn left to pass the hotel. At the road junction, cross over the Great Langdale road to a lane that passes by the end of the cottages. Follow the lane, ascending to intercept another road. Turn right for a short distance and then left towards Tarn Foot farm. Bear right along the track, in front of the cottages. Where the track splits, bear left. Through the gate carry on along the track to overlook Loughrigg Tarn. At a point half-way along the tarn cross the stile over the iron railings on the left.

③ Follow the footpath down the meadow to traverse right, just above the tarn. The footpath swings off right to climb a ladder stile over the stone wall. Follow the grassy track leading right, up

the hill, to a gate and stile on to the road. Turn left along the road, until a surfaced drive leads up to the right, signed 'Public Footpath Skelwith Bridge'. Pass a small cottage and keep on the track to pass a higher cottage, Crag Head. A little way above this, a narrow grassy footpath leads off right, up the hillside, to gain a level shoulder between the craggy outcrops of Little Loughrigg.

WHAT TO LOOK OUT FOR

Carrying the full contents of the River Brathay over a vertical drop of some 30ft (9m), Skelwith Force waterfall is an impressive sight. A little bridge provides access to the rocks above the force, and steps and a walkway lead to lower rocks and a good viewpoint. Access is unrestricted, though the rocks are polished and the waterfall unguarded. A weir once diverted water from above the falls to power the mills at Skelwith Bridge just downstream.

④ Cross the shoulder and descend the path, passing a little tarnlet to the right, to intercept a stone wall. Keep left along the wall descending to find, in a few hundred paces, a ladder stile leading over the wall into the upper woods of Rob Rash. A steep descent leads down to the road. Cross this directly, and go through the gap in the wall next to the large double gates. Descend a track to meet up with the outward route. Bear right to return to Elterwater village.

WHILE YOU'RE THERE

At Skelwith Bridge the path goes through the middle of a working slate finishing quarry. Although the rock is extracted from a quarry above Kirkstone Pass, it is sawn, split and polished here. It has many uses varying from practical roofing slates, to decorative panels for prestige buildings, to ornamental coffee tables. Some of the finished products can be viewed in the Touchstone Gallery below the works to the right of the path.

Overleaf: Footbridge, Watendlath Beck (Walk 23)

With Rogue Herries by Dock Tarn and Watendlath

From Stonethwaite to Rosthwaite through Herries country.

DISTANCE *7.5 miles (12.1km)*   **MINIMUM TIME** *3hrs 30min*

ASCENT/GRADIENT *1,102ft (336m)* ▲▲▲ **LEVEL OF DIFFICULTY** ✦✦✦

PATHS *Bridleways, fairly good paths and some rough walking*

LANDSCAPE *Fells, forest, tarns and lakes*

SUGGESTED MAP *OS Explorer OL4 The English Lakes (NW)*

START / FINISH *Grid reference: NY 262137*

DOG FRIENDLINESS *Sheep country; keep dogs under control*

PARKING *By telephone box in Stonethwaite*

PUBLIC TOILETS *Watendlath*

One stormy night in 1739, Francis 'Rogue' Herries brought his family to live in the house his grandfather built in Borrowdale. His son, David, 'woke again to see that all the horses were at a standstill and were gathered about a small stone bridge.' The 'hamlet... clustered beyond the bridge' was probably Grange. From there they crossed over a hill to come at last 'into a little valley, as still as a man's hand and bleached under the moon, but guarded by a ring of mountains that seemed to David gigantic.' This is the village of Rosthwaite and the Hazel Bank hotel sits on the spot where the Herries house stood. However, this house never existed except in the imagination of the novelist Hugh Walpole (1884–1941) and between the covers of the four volume series he wrote, collectively known as *The Herries Chronicle* (1930–33).

The Herries Family Saga

Walpole, one of the best-selling writers of his day, wrote over 50 novels. He bought a house above Derwent Water in 1923 and two years later announced that he was 'pinning all my hopes on two or three Lakes' novels, which will at least do something for this adorable place.' What he eventually produced over a five year period was a romantic history of a Lake District family from 1730 to 1932. Woven into the Herries' story are the major historic events of the period. The Jacobite Rebellion of 1745 passes near by in Carlisle, 'Rogue' Herries' son David dies at Uldale as the Bastille falls in 1789 and Judith, his daughter, gives birth to her son Adam in Paris as Napoleon is finally defeated in 1815.

'Rogue' Herries, soon notorious in Borrowdale for his wildness, completes his infamy by selling his mistress at a fair. His consuming, unrequited love for Mirabell Starr, a gypsy woman, drives him to wander the country for hundreds of miles in search of her, confirming his reputation as a strange character. Finally at Rosthwaite, after 44 years in Borrowdale, he dies as Judith, the daughter of his old age, is born in 1774. Walpole was once allegedly asked to adjudicate between two rival claimants as to which house in Watendlath Judith had lived in. He supposedly told one of them that not only had she not lived in his house, she had never lived anywhere. There is still a plaque on a farmhouse there, proclaiming the building to be the home of Judith Paris.

STONETHWAITE

However, the setting of the books is real enough and Walpole's evocative descriptions enrich the enjoyment of walking through his stones and skies. They capture the essence of this wild and beautiful place and convey the character of many of its inhabitants.

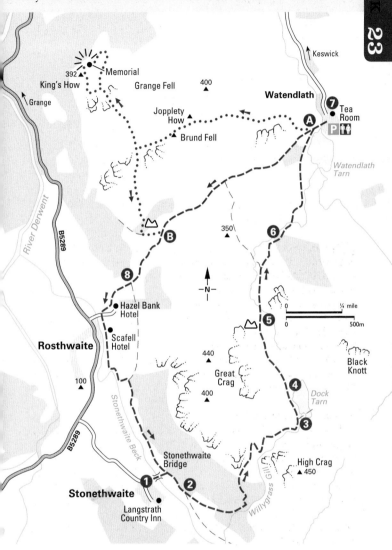

WALK 23 DIRECTIONS

❶ From the parking area in Stonethwaite, turn right and walk down the track to Stonethwaite Bridge. Cross it and go through a gate then turn right on to the bridleway to Grasmere. Go through another gate and after

about 250yds (229m), look for a path off to the left, through a gap in the low wall.

❷ Follow this path up through a wood, then cross a stile and continue uphill on a well-paved path through the trees. The path emerges from the trees still

WHERE TO EAT AND DRINK

The Langstrath Country Inn at Stonethwaite is just the place for an end-of-walk meal. Or you can relax with a pint and a bar meal in front of the log fire in the Scafell Hotel at Rosthwaite. But the number one choice has to be lunch in the tea room at Watendlath, where, on a fine day, you can eat outside.

climbing. Cross a stile beside Willygrass Gill and follow the path to Dock Tarn.

3 Ignore the track going right, over the beck, and continue on the obvious path around the left side of the tarn. There are some rocky sections but the going isn't difficult. If the lower path is flooded, higher paths to your left lead in the same direction.

4 At the north end of the tarn the broad path continues above boggy ground in the direction of a gap between two low crags. A view opens up ahead with Ether Knott then the Skiddaw beyond. Just past a small rock pinnacle on the left, Watendlath comes into view and the path descends a steep rocky staircase to a kissing gate.

5 Go through the gate, cross the beck and follow the green-topped wooden posts on a stone

WHAT TO LOOK OUT FOR

Just to the left of the pedestrian exit from the National Trust car park in Watendlath is a white farmhouse with a plaque on the wall proclaiming it to be the house of Walpole's fictional Judith Paris. Geese feed on the grass in front of the farm while ducks bob about in the water near the ancient packhorse bridge.

path across the bog. Turn right at a junction signed 'Watendlath' and descend to a sheep pen. Go through the gap in the wall and descend to a kissing gate.

6 Go through the gate, follow the stream downhill, cross it then follow the line of the wall round the field before turning left on to a farm track. Go through three gates and turn right across the old pack bridge into Watendlath.

7 From Watendlath re-cross the bridge and follow the bridleway sign to Rosthwaite. Walk uphill on this well-used route, go through a kissing gate and head downhill, passing a gate on the right and going through another gate, lower down. At the bottom of the hill a sign indicates that the path continues to Stonethwaite.

8 Ignore the sign and instead turn right through the gate in the wall, go downhill, pass through another gate beside Hazel Bank Hotel then turn left on to the public bridleway and follow this back to Stonethwaite Bridge.

WHILE YOU'RE THERE

The single track road to Watendlath from the Keswick to Borrowdale road is one of the most scenic in the Lake District. Half-way up you'll cross Ashness Bridge, with the much pictured backdrop of distant lakes and mountains (See Walk 29). Also worth seeing are the spectacular Lodore Falls, the subject of Robert Southey's famous poem *The Cataract of Lodore* (1820). He wrote 'How does the water come down at Lodore?' Formed by the water rushing down the beck from Watendlath Tarn and tumbling over some large stones, you'll find the falls just behind the Lodore hotel.

Over Grange Fell

*Extend the walk to take in one of the finest views
in the Lake District.*
See map and information panel for Walk 23

DISTANCE 6.75 miles (10.9km)   **MINIMUM TIME** 5hrs
ASCENT/GRADIENT 1,562ft (476m) ▲▲▲   **LEVEL OF DIFFICULTY** +++

WALK 24 DIRECTIONS
(Walk 23 option)

This area was acquired by the National Trust in 1910, the year of King Edward VII's death, and a memorial just below the summit of King's How reads: 'In loving memory of King Edward VII Grange Fell is dedicated by his sister Louise as a sanctuary of rest and peace, Here may all beings gather strength and find scenes of beautiful nature a cause for gratitude and love to God giving them courage and vigour to carry on his will'.

From the summit of King's How there is a glorious view to the north over Derwent Water to Keswick and Skiddaw. Closer, in the plain of the River Derwent, with the steep sides of Cat Bells and High Spy rising behind, lies the tiny hamlet of Grange, where in the first of the Herries chronicles, 'Rogue' Herries lifted from the water the body of the old woman they had drowned as a witch. The bridge from which they threw her is visible.

Leave the route of Walk 23 by the fingerpost for Rosthwaite and Dock Tarn (Point **Ⓐ**). Ignore both routes but pick up a faint path to the right, leading up to a gate in the wall. Go through this and continue up a narrow path between crags to a boggy area. Keep a wall on your right as you ascend towards Jopplety How. When you reach a crossing wall, bear left to locate a single ladder stile. Cross this and continue, around Jopplety How and up to the rocky little summit of Brund Fell. Beyond this, descend to a T-junction. Turn right and descend on an obvious path, crossing a wall by a ladder stile. Cross another stile over a fence and turn right, along the edge of a boggy valley.

At the far side, by a prominent yew tree, turn left and follow a rocky path that ascends the ridge of King's How. Pass the memorial to King Edward VII and continue over the summit, before descending on the far side, first along the ridge then dropping down to the left, back to the stile crossed earlier.

Re-trace your steps up to the T-junction and continue straight on, eventually descending very steeply by a wood to a gated stile. Over this turn left and ascend briefly to another gate, leading out on to the main Rosthwaite bridleway, (Point **Ⓑ**). Turn right and rejoin the route for Walk 23.

Art in Grizedale Forest

Wandering through Cumbria's only 'interactive' woods.

DISTANCE *5 miles (8km)* **MINIMUM TIME** *3hrs*

ASCENT/GRADIENT *820ft (250m)* ▲▲▲ **LEVEL OF DIFFICULTY** +++
(easier with trail map from information centre)

PATHS *Forest tracks and woodland paths, 3 stiles*

LANDSCAPE *Conifer plantations and mixed woodland*

SUGGESTED MAP *OS Explorer OL7 The English Lakes (SE)*

START / FINISH *Grid reference: SD 336944*

DOG FRIENDLINESS *Can run free inside forest boundaries*

PARKING *Several car parks at Grizedale Visitor Centre*

PUBLIC TOILETS *At Visitor Centre*

WALK 25 DIRECTIONS

Grizedale, 'the valley of the pigs', has always been forested, from the time when wild boar were hunted here by Norman barons, through to the present day, when 6,047 acres (2,447ha) have been covered, largely with conifers. Perhaps the guilt of planting all the Christmas trees got too much for the foresters in the 1970s. It was then that the 'art in the park' idea was born. There are now over 90 sculptures – round one corner there may be a wolf; round the next there's something that you can't quite comprehend, perhaps waiting for you to give it some meaning. You can even interact with the drums and marimbas that you'll see late in the walk.

The route follows the green waymarks of the Silurian Trail almost to Satterthwaite. Starting from the Visitor Centre, cut diagonally left across the play area, go through the doorway in the wall out on to a lane and turn right. Just beyond the farmhouse on the right, leave the lane for a path, which is highlighted by a waymark post. The path leaves and rejoins a cycle route before coming to a forestry road, where you turn right.

WHAT TO LOOK OUT FOR

The ancient oak woods around Bogle Crag once provided the charcoal for iron smelting. You may notice the old flattened hollows of the charcoal pitsteads. You will also see a restored potash pit beside the Bogle Trail.

Ignore the first path that doubles back left, then leave the forestry road for a track forking left. With a wall on the right and bracken and bramble on the left, the track climbs steadily uphill. After dipping to ford a couple of streams the route forks left and cuts across to the forestry road on the horizon. Turn left here and follow the road south, with Carron Crag's summit rock directly ahead. Where the track bends sharp left leave it to scale a stile in a deer fence. A little path now wriggles through trees and scrub to the summit trig point and the best viewpoint of the day. To the west, the Coniston fells are laid out across the horizon.

On the descent you'll see a large wood-carved ring, an exhibit by Linda Watson called 17° South. Seen from the path, it frames the village of Satterthwaite to perfection and makes a good seat to enjoy the view. The path continues to descend to rejoin the forestry road abandoned earlier. Just to the left you'll see a huge wooden statue, David Kemp's The Ancient Forester. Back at the junction, turn right along the forestry road to a crossroads of tracks, where you go straight ahead (south) on the green route. The track ends at a turning circle, but the route continues as a narrow path that weaves through lovely mixed woodland. Along this section you'll see a series of symbolic art, but it is less interesting than the beauty of the surroundings.

The path then descends to a forestry road. Turn right, then immediately left on the forest road, down into the gill and over the bridges. The track arcs left. Leave it for the waymarked path on the right, which passes a sheltered seat before rejoining the track further uphill. Continue with the green posts, dropping down to the left from the forest road. Leaving the forest the track becomes a narrow walled lane, Moor Lane, which comes out to the Satterthwaite road by a small car park.

Turn left along the lane into Satterthwaite, passing the inn and the church, before taking the second cul-de-sac on the right, up past the cemetery towards Bogle Wood. At the terminus take the left of two lilac-banded waymarkers (northbound), the Bogle Crag Trail. The path heads north through woodland. Ignore the path doubling back uphill at the next junction, and turn right on meeting the forestry road.

Where the Bogle Crag Trail climbs away to the right, go ahead on a winding forestry trail. Abandon this at a white waymarker for a narrow path on the left, which descends to join a tarmac path (blue waymarkers). Take the lower path at the next junction.

Pass beneath a huge footbridge, then double back left. Sculptures come thick and fast now. Paul Dodgson's, Shadow Faces of the Forest and Family Day Out are rather like Alberto Giacometti sculptures in wood. You may hear jungle music coming through the trees, and if you're lucky you can join in. First there's Jony Easterby's African Drums and Marimba, then there's Will Menter's Rabbit Hole Marimba. The route now weaves its way back past the new visitor facilities and the terraces of the old hall to the road just short of the Visitor Centre.

Taking the Line to Latrigg

A walk along a disused railway line, leads across the top of Latrigg to a fine viewpoint above Keswick.

WALK 26

DISTANCE 5 miles (8km)   **MINIMUM TIME** 2hrs

ASCENT/GRADIENT 902ft (275m) ▲▲▲   **LEVEL OF DIFFICULTY** ✦✦✦

PATHS Railway trackbed, country lane, grassy fell paths, 3 stiles

LANDSCAPE River valley and elongated grassy ridge

SUGGESTED MAP OS Explorer OL4 The English Lakes (NW)

START / FINISH Grid reference: NY 270238

DOG FRIENDLINESS No particular problems, but fell sheep on Latrigg

PARKING At former Keswick Station

PUBLIC TOILETS At start

The railway line from Penrith to Cockermouth was the only one to actually pass through this area, taking an intentional line to Keswick in order to tap into the tourist market. Opened to goods traffic in October 1864 and to passengers two months later, the line was, however, built for industrial rather than tourist reasons, to transport low phosphorous coke from Durham via Stainmore to the iron foundries of West Cumberland.

Strangely, in spite of having a profound impact on the development of the mining and industrial areas of Cumberland, the existence of Lakeland's railways was a brief one. Their development began in the 1840s, but by the 1970s only a single line around the Lakeland fringe remained – that, and a tentative link between Windermere and Kendal.

Thomas Bouch the engineer for the Cockermouth, Keswick and Penrith Railway, (known as the CK&P railway) tried to choose an easy route between Cockermouth and Penrith, but there were still many hollows to fill in, hills to tunnel and rivers to cross. There are 135 bridges on this 31-mile (50km) long railway line, eight of them over the River Greta.

Low Briery

One of the stops along the route was Low Briery, the site of an old bobbin mill. In the early 19th century there was a water-powered pencil mill here, several bobbin mills and a specialist textile mill, known locally as Fancy Bottoms Mill, which made the intricate bottom edgings of waistcoats.

The earliest bobbin mills in Cumbria appeared during the Industrial Revolution in response to demand from the mills of Lancashire and Yorkshire. By the mid-19th century, there were some 120 water-powered bobbin mills in the Lake District alone, producing half of all the bobbins required by the entire world textile industry. Bobbins from Low Briery, which at peak production could turn over 40 million bobbins a year, went as far as Central America, South Africa and Hong Kong. There were many different types of bobbin made at Low Briery, including those used for making the Coronation gown of Queen Elizabeth II. Other bobbins were used for silk, cotton, Irish linen and the wire that was inserted into the old pound notes.

LATRIGG

The arrival of the railway in 1864, meant that timber could be brought from further away and made it was easier for the growing workforce to reach the mill. However, with the decline of the textile industry and competition from abroad, the bobbin market collapsed, and Low Briery closed in 1961. By March 1972, the whole of this modest railway enterprise, too, came to an end. Much of the route has since been incorporated into the A66 road, but some remains as the Keswick Railway Footpath and a stretch of the National Cycle Network.

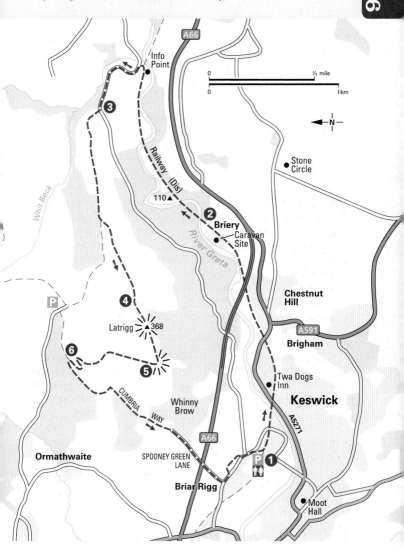

WALK 26 DIRECTIONS

❶ From the old Keswick Station, head along the trackbed, which speeds you away from Keswick. Beyond the A66, here cantilevered above the trackbed, the route covers a boardwalk section high above the River Greta, before continuing to the site of the bobbin mill at Low Briery, now a caravan site.

2 Beyond Low Briery, the River Greta is an agreeable companion as far as an old railway building on the right used as an information point (with a river bridge beyond). Before reaching the building, turn left through a gate and cross a narrow pasture to a back lane. Turn left and climb, steeply for a short while, to reach a footpath signed 'Skiddaw', at a gate and stile.

3 Go over the stile and on to a broad track swinging right round gorse bushes, and then running centrally up the eastern ridge of Latrigg. Look back here for spectacular views of surrounding fells. A short way on you reach a plantation on the right. Before the plantation ends, climb left from a

metal gate towards the top of the track and along the ridge to a gate.

4 After the gate, a lovely stroll leads across the top of Latrigg, with great views of the Vale of Keswick, the Dodds, Borrowdale, the Newlands Valley, and, to the right, the massive bulk of Skiddaw.

5 Beyond the highest point of Latrigg, a bench is perfectly placed to admire the view. From it take a path descending gently northwards, keeping left then dropping in zig-zags to intercept a track alongside another plantation.

6 At the track, turn left, and continue down to Spooney Green Lane, which crosses high above the A66 and runs on to meet Briar Rigg, a back lane. At this junction, turn left into Briar Rigg, and follow the lane (an enclosed path on the left along Briar Rigg makes for safer passage), until you can branch right at a pronounced left bend to return to the car park.

Avoiding the Old Man

A mountain route on Swirl How avoids the hordes
on the nearby Old Man.

DISTANCE *8 miles (12.9km)*   **MINIMUM TIME** *5hrs*

ASCENT/GRADIENT *2,820ft (860m)* ▲▲▲   **LEVEL OF DIFFICULTY** +++

PATHS *Well-defined mountain paths and tracks, no stiles*

LANDSCAPE *High mountain*

SUGGESTED MAP *OS Explorer OL6 The English Lakes (SW)*

START / FINISH *Grid reference: SD 303975*

DOG FRIENDLINESS *Off lead on mountain ridges*
but sheep graze Prison Band in summer

PARKING *Pay-and-display near Coniston church*

PUBLIC TOILETS *At car park*

NOTE *Walk not advised in poor visiblity*

The Old Man of Coniston's too busy: he's always too busy at weekends and in summer. Swirl How's only a couple feet lower at 2,630ft, and if you've gone metric they're the same – 803m above sea level. We'll try Swirl How instead. Coniston is the best place to start. The mountains show their finest rock faces to Coniston. Once you're through the green fields and woods surrounding the village the walk deposits you in a huge stadium of broken stone. In it, grassed-over spoil heaps, mill races and mysterious flooded mine shafts all lie in the shadow of quarry-terraced mountainsides.

Fool's Copper

Though copper mining here dates back to Roman times, large-scale mining began some 400 years ago. It reached its peak in the mid-19th century before going into decline in the 1870s. The hard rock of the Borrowdale volcanic group made the drilling difficult and slow and the sound of gunpowder explosions would have echoed round the valley. Some of the veins were over 1,000ft (305m) below ground and over 500ft (152m) below sea level. The miners could only access the veins by wooden ladders and staging platforms that were used for the tramming of the ore. The ore was known as chalcopyrite (sulphide of copper and iron), which has a yellow/gold colour, not unlike 'fool's gold'.

Today, the deep shafts are flooded and they are far too dangerous for serious exploration. Rock debris has fallen down on to the old wooden platforms and as a result it's difficult to tell whether you're standing on the floor of the pit or trusting your fate to rotten timber.

Beyond the mines you pass Levers Water, a natural tarn enlarged and dammed by the miners for a supply reservoir. The excitement begins at the pass of Swirl Hawse. From here climbing the Prison Band takes you into rocky terrain – steep, but not serious enough for the use of hands. Soon you're at the huge summit cairn looking across the grassy whaleback of Brim Fell to the Old Man. Chances are you'll see a hundred little silhouettes: walkers shuffling about against the backdrop of a Morecambe Bay skyline. We could go there now – it's easy.

SWIRL HOW

But an afterthought at this stage is never worthwhile, so we'll continue with our route for purists and connoisseurs, taking the little path that rakes across the high sides of Brim Fell. It comes out at Goat's Hawse, a boulder pass with a wonderful view of the magnificent climbers' cliffs and buttresses of Dow Crag away to your right. And what more fitting way to end the walk than on Walna Scar Road, where the Romans transported their copper ore, over the mountains to the port of Ravenglass.

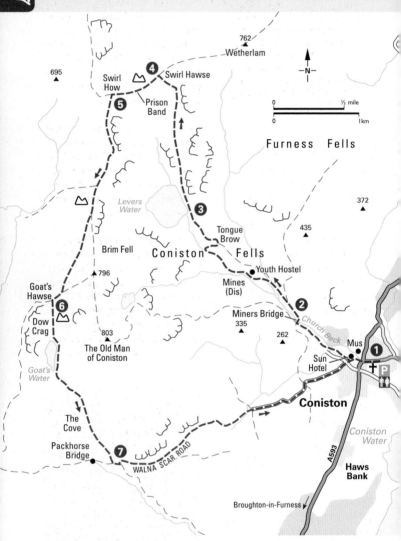

WALK 27 DIRECTIONS

1 Turn left out of the main car park in Coniston to pass St Andrew's Church, then left again in the village centre, before taking the first right up Walna Scar Road. After passing the Sun Hotel go right to follow a path which traces Church Beck to the old Miners Bridge above some dramatic waterfalls.

SWIRL HOW

② Cross the bridge and turn left alongside the beck. The track comes to the vast area of the Coniston copper mines, and passes beneath some terraced cottages before swinging left behind the youth hostel. At the next junction, take the right fork, above Paddy End water treatment works, ascending the slopes of Tongue Brow to Levers Water.

③ From here the track becomes a path, climbing steadily up to the high pass of Swirl Hawse, which separates the summits of Swirl How and Wetherlam.

④ On reaching the pass, turn left and climb up a rough path that weaves and scrambles over the rocks of the Prison Band to reach the cairn on Swirl How's summit.

⑤ Continue along the cairned ridge path, descending to a saddle between Swirl How and the grassy whaleback of Brim Fell. Keep watch for a narrow path branching off to the right. This rounds the high sides of Brim Fell for a direct route to Goat's Hawse, the pass overlooking Goat's Water.

⑥ On reaching the pass, descend towards Goat's Water, passing beneath the cliffs of Dow Crag. A rough and rocky route traces the eastern shores of the tarn before swinging left into the grassy bowl known as The Cove.

⑦ The path meets the Walna Scar Road just beyond the Cove Beck packhorse bridge. Turn left to follow the ancient road round the south sides of the Old Man. In the lower regions, the road becomes a tarmac, hedge-lined lane, descending to the Sun Hotel and back into the village centre.

Overleaf: Derwent Water from Walla Crag (Walk 28)

Keswick's Walla Crag Above Derwent Water

Wonderful panoramas to the surrounding fells, a jewelled lake and sylvan splendour are the delights of this walk.

DISTANCE 5.25 miles (8.4km)   **MINIMUM TIME** 3hrs

ASCENT/GRADIENT 1,083ft (330m) ▲▲▲ **LEVEL OF DIFFICULTY** +++

PATHS Good paths and tracks, steep ascent and descent, 3 stiles

LANDSCAPE Woods, open fell and lakeside

SUGGESTED MAP OS Explorer OL4 The English Lakes (NW)

START / FINISH Grid reference: NY 265229

DOG FRIENDLINESS Fields and open fell grazed by sheep, open lakeside, suitable for dogs under control

PARKING Derwent Head pay-and-display car park

PUBLIC TOILETS At Derwent Head, above lake

At the foot of Borrowdale, often referred to as the most beautiful valley in England, the northern head of Derwent Water opens to Keswick and the northern fells with dramatic effect. While experiencing the considerable charm of the woods and lakeside, the highlight of this walk is undeniably the staggering view from the heights of Walla Crag. West across Derwent Water, beyond Cat Bells, Maiden Moor and the secretive Newland Valley, stand the striking north western fells of Causey Pike, Sail, Crag Hill and Grisedale Pike. To the south-west rise Glaramara and Great Gable. To the north Skiddaw and Blencathra. Undeniably one of the most evocative viewpoints within the whole of the Lake District National Park.

Tank Manoeuvres

This walk touches the lake shore before traversing the oak woods of Cockshot and Castlehead, to rise to the craggy top of Castle Head. A fine viewpoint in its own right, guarded on three sides by steep crags, it is reputedly the site of an Iron Age hill-fort. Springs Wood follows before ascent can be made to the steep open shoulder leading to Walla Crag. The metal strips seen in the track once provided grip for the caterpillar tracks of tanks on training manoeuvres here during the Second World War. Before the latest metric surveys by the Ordnance Survey the height of Walla Crag was easy to remember – it was 1,234ft above sea level! Descent through Great Wood follows and a delectable stroll home along the shore of this beautiful lake.

Derwent Water

The lake is 3 miles (4.8km) long and 72ft (22m) deep and is fed by the River Derwent. A speed limit ensures that motor powered boats do not ply its waters. Seasonal salmon, brown trout, Arctic char, perch and the predatory pike swim beneath the surface.

There are four islands on the lake, all owned by the National Trust. The largest and most northerly of the four is Derwent Isle. Once owned by Fountains Abbey it was bought by German miners from the Company of Mines Royal in 1569. The island and part of its grand 18th-century house are open to visitors on a handful of days during the year. St Herbert's Island was reputedly home to the Christian missionary of that name in the 10th century and monks remained in residence after his departure. A ruinous summer house is all that stands there today.

By the path, just above Derwent Bay, is an inscribed slate plaque in honour of Canon H D Rawnsley who did much to keep the lake as it remains today. He was vicar of Crosthwaite, the parish church of Keswick, from 1883 to 1917, and was one of Lakeland's greatest conservationists. In 1895 he became a co-founder of the National Trust. He was a campaigner against rude postcards and also encouraged Beatrix Potter to publish her first book *The Tale of Peter Rabbit* in 1900.

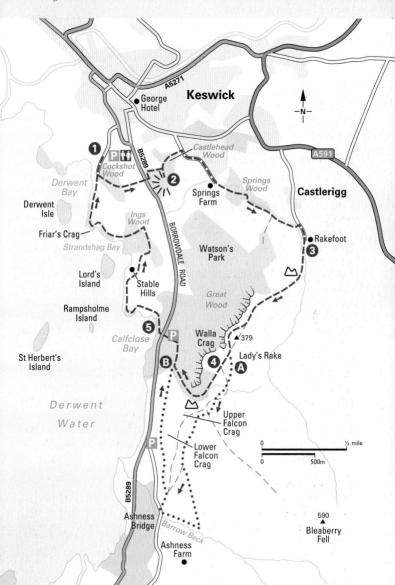

WALK 28 DIRECTIONS

1 Proceed down the road to Derwent Bay. Go left opposite the landing stages, past the toilets, to take the track through Cockshot Wood. Exit the wood on to a fenced lane which leads across the field to the Borrowdale road. Cross the road and climb the stone steps to enter Castlehead Wood. Take the path which trends left to ascend the shoulder. In a little way a steeper path climbs up to the right, to the rocky summit of Castle Head and a fine viewpoint.

WHAT TO LOOK OUT FOR

The rocky knoll of Friar's Crag, with its stand of Scots pine, is a most famous lakeside viewpoint. At the foot of the crag, attached to the rocks which are often submerged when the lake level is high, memorial plaques detail all the former mayors of Keswick.

2 Descend by the same route to the shoulder then bear right to locate a kissing gate into an enclosed lane. Follow this to Springs Road and turn right. When you reach Springs Farm, cross a bridge and take the track up through Springs Wood. Bear right at the junction and follow the edge of the wood up past the TV mast. Ignore a turning on the right and continue to a footbridge left to join Castlerigg Road. Turn right along the road and walk up past Rakefoot to another footbridge on the right.

3 Cross the footbridge over the stream and follow the path, ascending by the stone wall. Go through a gate, and walk out on to the open shoulder of the fell, ascending the steep grassy nose. The going levels until a gate on the right, through the wall,

leads to a path which follows the edge of the crag. Caution, there is a steep unfenced drop. Those wishing to stay away from the cliff edge can take a higher stile. Follow the path, which crosses the head of a gully, to climb on to the polished rock cap of Walla Crag where the views are superb.

WHERE TO EAT AND DRINK

In Keswick you'll find the George Hotel, the town's oldest inn, which serves Jennings real ales and has both restaurant and bar meal facilities. There is also a café overlooking Derwent Bay.

4 Continue along the main ridge path down to a stile over the wall. Cross and go right, down the hill following a grassy path which becomes increasingly steep and stepped into the gorge of Cat Gill. Entering Great Wood continue steeply down, passing a bridge (Point **B**, Walk 29) before leaving the beck to head into the wood. Bear left down the hill, across a wooded car park and on, to locate a gap in the wall on the Borrowdale Road. Cross to the gap in the wall opposite and continue to the lakeshore.

5 Bear right, following around Calfclose Bay, by Stable Hills, around Ings Wood and Strandshag Bay to the Scots pine on Friar's Crag. Continue easily back to Derwent Bay and take the footpath along the road to the car park.

WHILE YOU'RE THERE

The Derwentwater Motor Launch Company runs regular sailings around the lake. Landing stages en route include Ashness Gate, Lodore, High Brandlehow, Low Brandlehow, Hawes End and Nichol End.

To Ashness Bridge

Make the most of the magnificent views over Derwent Water and visit Ashness Bridge.

See map and information panel for Walk 28

DISTANCE 7 miles (11.3km)   **MINIMUM TIME** 3hrs 45min

ASCENT/GRADIENT 1,150ft (350m) ▲▲▲   **LEVEL OF DIFFICULTY** +++

WALK 29 DIRECTIONS
(Walk 28 option)

This high level extension, which makes a gradual descent down open fellside to Ashness Bridge, provides a fine open vista over Derwent Water. Steep hillside and vertical crags lay below the path and this is not a route for an undisciplined group or when visibility is poor.

From the summit of Walla Crag, follow the main path down to the stile and cross back into open country (Point Ⓐ). Turn left and walk downhill a few paces before picking out a grassy track striking off left, traversing the boggy ground surrounding the head of Cat Gill. The path crosses another little tributary before it rounds a shoulder and begins a gradual descent in the direction of Ashness Farm. Ignore a track off down to the right and continue descending gradually to a pair of gates by a wall junction. Go through the left-hand gate and descend more steeply, making a sharp right turn down to a gate alongside Barrow Beck. Go through the gate and descend to the road to admire Ashness Bridge.

The view down over the bridge to Derwent Water with Skiddaw beyond, is quite magnificent and is, perhaps, the most popular calendar photograph in the Lake District. It is particularly fine in autumn when the leaves of a stand of silver birch below, colour lemon to golden yellow. This type of stone arch bridge is a noted feature of Lakeland. Traditionally the bridges were built without concrete or mortar to keep the materials in place. It is the weight of the stones, thrusting against a central keystone of the arch, that holds the bridge together. In construction a carpenter would form a temporary wooden arch and the stones, usually from the beck itself, were simply laid on this. Once the keystone was placed the timbers were removed and the arch supported itself.

Now turn right, down the road, for 100yds (91m) before picking up a track on the right, rising to a gate. Go through the gate and take the left fork towards Keswick. Traverse beneath the cliffs of Lower Falcon Crag and the next higher cliff, Upper Falcon Crag, keeping along the high track, which contours the hillside, without losing height. This leads to a bridge over Cat Gill and a junction with Walk 28 at Point Ⓑ in Great Wood. Follow this through Point ❺ to return to the car park at the start.

Spectacular Hodge Close

Explore Little Langdale and the gaping hole of Hodge Close Quarry.

DISTANCE 4.5 miles (7.2km)	**MINIMUM TIME** 2hrs
ASCENT/GRADIENT 623ft (190m) ▲▲▲	**LEVEL OF DIFFICULTY** +++

PATHS Stony paths and tracks, road, 5 stiles

LANDSCAPE Disused slate quarries, village below high fells, wooded dales, little river

SUGGESTED MAP OS Explorer OL7 The English Lakes (SE)

START / FINISH Grid reference: SD 316017

DOG FRIENDLINESS Generally good; sheep grazing and short road section

PARKING On Hodge Close Quarry Bank by roadside

PUBLIC TOILETS None en route; nearest at Coniston

WALK 30 DIRECTIONS

From Yewdale the quiet vale of Tilberthwaite corkscrews northwards between brackened and craggy fells into a narrow wooded corridor that reaches the River Brathay in picturesque Little Langdale. A predominance of thick oak and deciduous woods cloak the valley flanks and bottom. Within these woods old slate quarries litter the landscape, bearing testament to a once prosperous industry.

This walk begins by the great hole of Hodge Close Quarry and proceeds by the hamlet of the same name to follow the high level route to Stang End Farm. Descent

WHERE TO EAT AND DRINK

The old Blacksmiths Cottage in the hamlet of Hodge Close sometimes serves teas in the summer months. Passed en route the Three Shires Inn in Little Langdale offers real ales, bar meals, afternoon teas and ice cream.

leads to Little Langdale and a crossing of the River Brathay. The route through the heart of the village leads on to the famous Slaters Bridge.

From the parking area follow the road down into the hamlet of Hodge Close. Hodge Close Quarry to the right, last worked in the early 1970s, is a huge gaping hole in the ground. It is unfenced, around 100ft (30m) deep and great caution should be exercised if approaching the edge. Although the edges of the quarry frequently peel away due to the slatey cleavage of the rock, it is a popular recreation area and stones must never be thrown into the workings. Often hidden from above, below the rim rock climbers scale the heights and divers explore the depths of the deep sump of water.

The road continues as a track, though it is classed as a public road and is used daily by the postman in his van. First pass through the hamlet of Hodge Close, then

LITTLE LANGDALE

WHAT TO LOOK OUT FOR

Hodge Close Quarry, which extends into Parrock Quarry through a great rock archway, is reputedly one of the largest artificial holes in England. Apart from its visible extent, the great water-filled sump, some 100ft (30m) deep, leads through tunnels to great underground chambers, known as Close Head Quarries. Local folklore tells of Jim Birkett, then apprentice river, or splitter, of the slate, who in the 1930s travelled the length of the quarry hanging by one hand from the jib of an aerial ropeway.

continue to pass cottages and on through a gate before descending into the woods. Keep along, then rise to pass through a gate and exit the wood. Fields open out below, before a rise beneath a craggy outcrop leads through another gate and into woods once again. Locally these are known as Sepulchre Wood and it is said that plague victims who died in Little Langdale were once buried here. One further gate leads to a short descent to Stang End.

Bear left to find a gate immediately to the left of the end cottage. Pass through the gate and follow the lane down between the stone walls. The track opens into a field with a gate and stile. Follow the path descending and crossing the field, often flooded, to cross the Lang Parrock footbridge spanning the River Brathay. There are steps at both ends of this narrow bridge. Ascend the field and take the gate out on to the road. Go left up the road through the centre of Little Langdale to pass the Three Shires Inn. The inn is named after the Three Shires Stone which stands near the summit of Wrynose Pass, where Lancashire and the old counties

of Westmorland and Cumberland met. Climb to the junction and turn left down the hill. Pass the white house of Low Birk How to reach steps and a gate leading off up to the right.

Follow the path up through the field to a gate. Keep along the narrow path beneath the rocks until it drops to bend around a stone wall and descends to Slaters Bridge. Cross the bridge and the stile beyond to continue until a further stile leads on to a track. Go right to pass Low Hall Garth and rise steeply past High Hall Garth. The track leads through a gate and fords a stream. Make a gradual ascent to a junction in a few hundred paces. Go left, up the track and over the high shoulder of Knotts. The route is straightforward and eventually descends into the farmyard of High Tilberthwaite.

Go left, initially rising over a rocky outcrop, to follow the low level track back along the valley. Beyond a gate the way leads over quarry banks before entering woods and making a curving descent to the right. At the bottom of the hill turn right at the junction and continue along this track to cross the stream of Pierce How Beck by a slab bridge. Ascend through the woods, passing beneath banks of quarry waste, before ascending to the hamlet of Hodge Close. Go right to the parking area.

WHILE YOU'RE THERE

Slaters Bridge is a popular attraction in Little Langdale. It spans the River Brathay with two great slabs of slate and a stone arch. It has been speculated that the narrow arch portion of the bridge may be of Roman origin.

D'ye Ken John Peel?

A visit to the killing fields of legendary huntsman John Peel.

DISTANCE 7.5 miles (12.1km)   MINIMUM TIME 4hrs

ASCENT/GRADIENT 1,213ft (370m) ▲▲▲ LEVEL OF DIFFICULTY +++

PATHS *Country lanes, bridle paths, good footpaths and some very rocky difficult walking through Burntod Gill*

LANDSCAPE *Fells, fields and lakes*

SUGGESTED MAP *OS Explorer OL4 The English Lakes (NW)*

START / FINISH *Grid reference: NY 230322*

DOG FRIENDLINESS *Under control in sheep country, particularly at lambing*

PARKING *Street parking in Bassenthwaite village*

PUBLIC TOILETS *None en route*

This part of the Lakes, at the 'Back o' Skiddaw' across the fells of Uldale and neighbouring Caldbeck, is where John Peel and his pack of hounds galloped in pursuit of foxes. Although possibly the world's most famous huntsman, he was far removed from the stereotypical red-coated country gentleman. Peel was a tall, rough spoken Cumbrian farmer with a loud voice. His coat of grey was made from everyday cloth. He wore knee britches, long stockings and shoes and a battered, well-worn beaver hat. To complete his outfit he carried a riding crop and a hunting horn. He liked nothing better than to spend a long day riding to hounds with his companions, returning home at dusk for a simple meal. Then they'd sit round the fire and indulge in an evening of heavy drinking before falling asleep in their chairs only to rise at dawn for another day on the fells.

John Peel was born at Caldbeck in 1776. At the age of 20 he fell in love with an Uldale girl called Mary White. They arranged to be married but when it came time for the banns to be read out in church, Mary's mother forbade the wedding because, 'They're far ower young'. Undeterred, Peel rode to Mary's house at midnight. She escaped from her bedroom window and they made for Gretna Green where they were married 'over the anvil' by the village blacksmith. Mary's mother accepted the situation and the marriage was ratified in the church at Caldbeck in December 1797.

Mary inherited a property in Ruthwaite where the family lived and farmed. However, John Peel had taken to hunting at an early age and married life did not interrupt his ardent pursuit of the fox. He died in 1854 and was buried in Caldbeck churchyard.

That would have been the end of the story had not his friend John Woodcock Graves, written a song about Peel. To the tune of *Bonnie Annie*, he dashed off *D'ye Ken John Peel*. He joked, 'By jove Peel, you'll be sung when we're both run to earth'. Peel might still have been consigned to oblivion had not William Metcalfe, choir master at Carlisle Cathedral, composed and published a new tune for the song in 1868. The following year he was invited to sing it at the annual dinner of the Cumberland Benevolent Institution in London. The song became popular and is now known throughout the world.

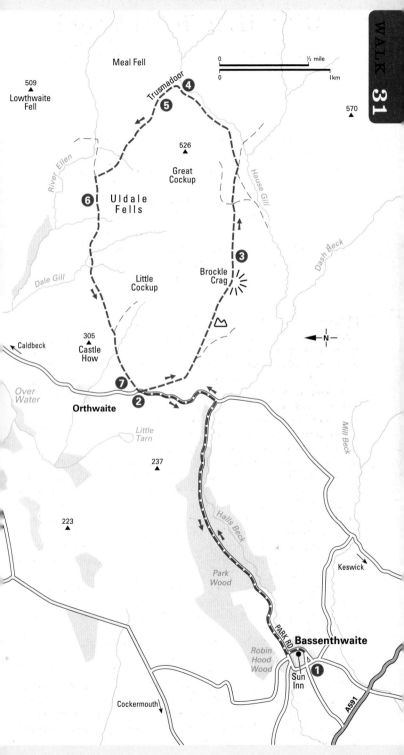

Meal Fell

509 ▲
Lowthwaite
Fell

Trusmadoor ❹

❺

570 ▲

526 ▲

Great
Cockup

River Ellen

Hause Gill

❻ U l d a l e
F e l l s

Dash Beck

❸

Brockle
Crag

Dale Gill

Little
Cockup

← N —

← Caldbeck

305 ▲
Castle
How

❼
❷

Orthwaite

Over
Water

Little
Tarn

237 ▲

Mill Beck

223 ▲

Halls Beck

Park
Wood

Keswick →

PARK RD

Bassenthwaite

Robin
Hood
Wood

❶

Sun
Inn

A591

Cockermouth ↓

½ mile

0   1 km

W
A
L
K

31

WALK 31 DIRECTIONS

❶ From the centre of Bassenthwaite village, pass the Sun Inn and turn right into Park Road. Follow this for 1.25 miles (2km) to a T-junction, with a signpost pointing to Orthwaite, and turn left. Continue for about 650yds (594m) to a junction with a farm road coming in from the right at a public footpath sign.

❷ Turn right, go along the road and through a gate signed 'Uldale Commons'. Follow the farm road to a public bridleway sign on the left. Take the bridleway and head uphill. It's a fairly steep climb to Brockle Crag before it levels out.

WHAT TO LOOK OUT FOR

When you emerge from Burntod Gill into the pass of Trusmadoor. It's a strange little pass, which Wainright described as 'the Piccadilly Circus of sheep in that locality'. Shepherds use this route to move flocks from pastures on one side of Great Cockup to the other with the sheep.

❸ The bridleway heads downhill, but before you reach a beck, strike off left on a sheep trod to the prominent stone-walled field. From here follow the narrow valley of Burntod Gill. The path is narrow and precarious in places.

❹ At the first notch in the hillside on the left, beside a cone-shaped knoll, head up to the left away from the water through the dry pass of Trusmadoor, between Great Cockup and Meal Fell.

WHERE TO EAT AND DRINK

Bassenthwaite is a small village with only one hostelry, but it's a topper. The Sun Inn has a reputation for serving excellent bar meals and a selection of real ales, both of which can be enjoyed in front of a log fire. If your taste is a bit more up-market, try the Castle Inn Hotel just outside the village.

❺ Coming through the pass, bear left across the head of a small stream to pick up another sheep trod, this one marked by an obvious line of reeds. Contour around the shoulder of the fell until you intersect a path coming up from the left. Bear left on this to round the shoulder of the fell.

❻ Ahead of you on the horizon is Castle How with a halo of Scots pine. To the left of this a wide path is seen going through the heather. Cross the fell to join this path and where the track forks, keep left.

❼ Eventually you will see a clump of trees in front and to the right and Bassenthwaite Lake to the left. Keep on this line and when the path fades follow the stone wall, returning to the farm road where you turn right then left down the minor road retracing your steps into Bassenthwaite village.

WHILE YOU'RE THERE

Beside the A591 are the grounds of 17th-century Mirehouse, which lead down to the shores of Bassenthwaite Lake and incorporate adventure playgrounds and a tea room set in the former sawmill. The house contains fine collections of furniture, literary portraits and manuscripts reflecting the family friendships with Tennyson, artist Francis Bacon, and historian and essayist Thomas Carlyle.

Ancient Oaks of Ard Crags

Try and imagine the Lakeland fells as they were before people arrived.

DISTANCE 5 miles (8km)   **MINIMUM TIME** 2hrs 30min

ASCENT/GRADIENT 1,306ft (398m) ▲▲▲   **LEVEL OF DIFFICULTY** +++

PATHS Road, narrow fell paths, one vague turning, stiles

LANDSCAPE Heathery ridge flanked by steep slopes

SUGGESTED MAP OS Explorer OL4 The English Lakes (NW)

START / FINISH Grid reference: NY 229201

DOG FRIENDLINESS On lead on road and on fell if sheep are grazing

PARKING Small car park in old roadside quarry at Rigg Beck

PUBLIC TOILETS None en route; nearest at Braithwaite and Buttermere

---

On this walk you can enjoy views of craggy fells and fine ridges. The landscape is very open, with gentle fields giving way to steeper slopes covered in bracken and heather. It's tempting to believe that the Lake District was always like this; bare, barren and wild. In fact, the natural state of the Lakeland fells, if humans had never set foot there or brought grazing livestock into the area, would be quite different. The climax vegetation would be deciduous forest, comprising oak and birch on most slopes, with alder in the boggy lowlands and rowan in the rocky clefts, leaving only the summits of the fells rising bare above the trees.

If it's hard to imagine what this kind of forest cover would look like, then study the patchy oak woods on the steep southern slopes of Ard Crags and Causey Pike. Short, gnarled oaks in these locations are thought to represent the last remaining indigenous Lakeland forests. They are sessile oaks, meaning that the acorn cups sit on the twigs, rather than pedunculate oaks, where the acorn cups are on stalks. The National Trust acorn logo, displayed all over the Lake District, shows a pedunculate oak.

Grazing Sheep

Centuries of sheep grazing have led to the Lake District's current appearance; a process accelerated when distant monasteries encouraged large-scale grazing from the 12th century. Constant nibbling prevents woodland cover from regenerating, so that established trees simply get older and eventually die. Their fruit can find no safe place to germinate unless protected from livestock and rabbits. Holly, hawthorn, gorse and brambles survive simply because they are so prickly, and many fine specimens of gorse can still be seen even on the sheep-grazed slopes on this walk.

While most walkers are keen to preserve the wilderness, it's likely that very few walkers would be happy with the Lake District if livestock were totally excluded, if blanket tree cover was allowed to re-establish itself. Gone would be the glorious views, replaced instead by dense woodland cover. Gone would be the fell paths, gradually choked by rampant vegetation and covered by drifts of leaf mould. In the case of Ard Crags, you wouldn't be able to enjoy the purple flush of heather that makes a walk along its ridge a joy in high summer.

The View

Ard Crags, surrounded by plenty of loftier summits, isn't a particularly high fell but the view is interesting. The ridge is a splendid perch for studying the patchwork landscape of the Vale of Newlands. Although the fells around the head of Newlands rise higher than Ard Crags, you can see the highest Lakeland fells, including the Scafells, Helvellyn and Skiddaw, as well as groups of fells around Ennerdale, Buttermere, Wasdale and Langdale.

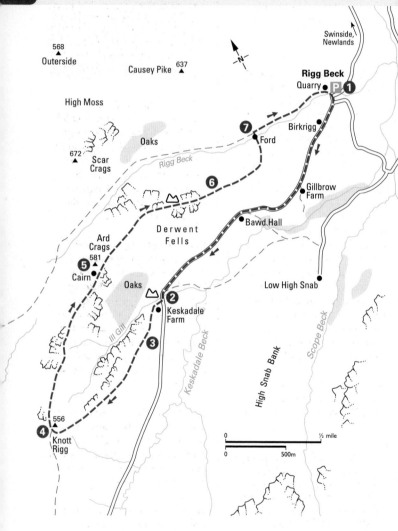

WALK 32 DIRECTIONS

1 Leave the quarry car park at Rigg Beck and walk up the road. Keep right at a junction and rise gently past farms and fields. Pass Birkrigg Farm and Newlands Fell, Gillbrow Farm and Bawd Hall. The road later descends gently across a more rugged fellside and reaches a sharply pronounced bend crossing the beck of Ill Gill. A steep slope covered in ancient sessile oaks rises to your right.

② Immediately after crossing the beck, locate a faint track steeply ascending the bank on your right. Just beyond the earthwork of a new farm steading above Keskadale Farm, cross a stile, and follow the faint path up the ridge to another stile. The path swings left briefly before zig-zagging steeply up the ridge.

③ The path is narrow as it crosses a steep, heathery slope, and there are some stony patches. Higher up the slope is boggy and the path is vague. Look up to the right to spot a gentle, rounded summit and aim for it. A small pile of stones sits on top. This is Knott Rigg at 1,824ft (556m), surrounded by higher fells.

④ A clear path heads roughly north-east along the hummocky ridge. Mosses, sedges and rushes

indicate wet ground. The path drops to a gap, then climbs uphill slightly to the right of the ridge. The ground cover is now heather, indicating drier ground. Gullies fall away to the right then the summit cairn on Ard Crags is reached, at 1,906ft (581m) the high point of this walk.

⑤ Walking along the heathery ridge is like walking on top of the world, with a fine view over the Vale of Newlands. Bilberry and crowberry grow among the heather, providing an autumn feed for birds or passing walkers. The descent is in two stages, dropping first to a heathery bump, and then dropping more steeply past outcrops of rock.

⑥ Heather gives way to bracken as the gradient eases, then the path runs level on to a blunt, grassy ridge. Swing left to descend alongside a wall and fence, where the slope is wet and boggy. At Rigg Beck ford the flow. If a narrower crossing point is needed, look a short way upstream.

⑦ Climb up from Rigg Beck and join a clear path, turning right to follow it down the valley. The slopes are covered in bracken with occasional clumps of gorse. The path leads back to the car park.

Cat Bells and High Spy

*A delightful romp high above two lovely valleys steeped
in industrial history culminates in views over Derwent Water.*

DISTANCE 9 miles (14.5km) **MINIMUM TIME** 4hrs

ASCENT/GRADIENT 2,460ft (750m) ▲▲▲ **LEVEL OF DIFFICULTY** +++

PATHS Generally good paths, indistinct above Tongue Gill, 4 stiles

LANDSCAPE Fell ridge tops, quarry workings, woodland, riverside path

SUGGESTED MAP OS Explorer OL4 The English Lakes (NW)

START / FINISH Grid reference: NY 247212

DOG FRIENDLINESS No special problems, though fell sheep roam tops

PARKING Wooded parking area at Hawes End

PUBLIC TOILETS None en route

NOTE Walk not advised in poor visibility

Both Borrowdale and the Newlands Valley, like many parts of Lakeland, have seen extensive periods of industry from an early age. From the top of Maiden Moor, scree can be seen issuing from the workings of an old mine in Newlands. This is Goldscope, a name that first appears in records during the reign of Elizabeth I, who imported German miners to work here. The name is a corruption of 'Gottesgab' or 'God's gift', so called because it was one of the most prosperous mines in Lakeland.

Copper was mined here as early as the 13th century from a vein 9ft (2.7m) thick. The mine also produced large quantities of lead, a small amount of silver and a modicum of gold. The mine's greatest period of production was in the 16th century, when Elizabeth made a serious attempt to exploit England's own resources to reduce dependency on imports. Ironically, it was German miners who largely worked Goldscope, encouraged by the award of hidden subsidies in the form of waived taxes. Copper ore was taken by packhorse to the shores of Derwent Water by way of Little Town. It was then transported to a smelter on the banks of the River Greta, at Brigham. From here the copper went to the Receiving House, now the Moot Hall, in Keswick, to receive the Queen's Mark.

The Rigghead Quarries in Tongue Gill produced slate from levels cut deep into the fellside and a number of adits are still open, though they are dangerous and should not be explored. But the real secret of these fells is wad, more commonly known as graphite, plumbago or black cawke – or the lead in your pencil. Its discovery dates from the early 16th century when trees uprooted in a storm revealed a black mineral on their roots. Shepherds soon realised that the substance was useful for marking sheep, and later for making metal castings and as a lubricant. Its other uses included a fixing agent for blue dyes, glazing pottery, a rust preventative, polishing iron and for casting shells and cannon balls.

Pencils, for which graphite was ultimately used, appeared around 1660 as wooden sticks with a piece of graphite in the tip. Keswick became the world centre of the graphite and pencil industries and the first record of a pencil factory appears in 1832. The Cumberland Pencil Company was first set up in nearby Braithwaite in 1868 and moved to its present site in Keswick 30 years later.

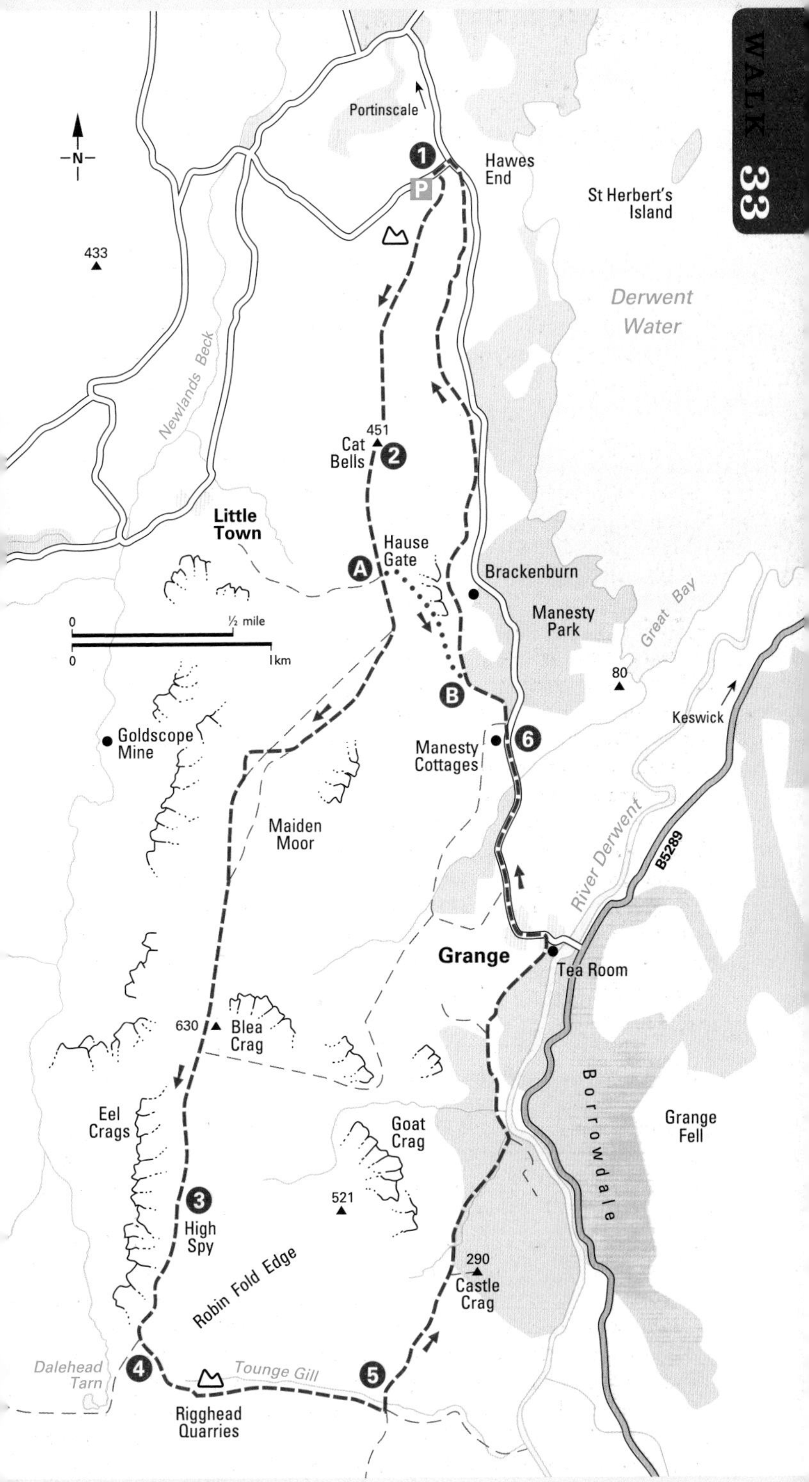

CAT BELLS

Portinscale

Hawes End

St Herbert's Island

Derwent Water

P

433 ▲

Newlands Beck

451 ▲
Cat Bells ②

Little Town

Hause Gate Ⓐ

Brackenburn

Manesty Park

Great Bay

Keswick

Goldscope Mine

Ⓑ

80 ▲

Maiden Moor

Manesty Cottages ⑥

0   ½ mile
0   1 km

Grange

Tea Room

630 ▲ Blea Crag

Eel Crags

Robin Fold Edge

Goat Crag

521 ▲

River Derwent

B5289

B o r r o w d a l e

Grange Fell

③ High Spy

290 ▲ Castle Crag

Dalehead Tarn ④   Tounge Gill   ⑤

Rigghead Quarries

WALK 33 DIRECTIONS

❶ At Hawes End, walk up the road and at a bend take a stepped and rocky path rising steeply. Follow this, climbing through small rocky outcrops before reaching Brandlehow. The onward route keeps to the centre of a grassy ridge, before rising through more rock outcrops to Cat Bells.

❷ From Cat Bells descend easily to the broad col of Hause Gate. This is Point Ⓐ, where the shorter Walk 34 branches left. Go forward across Hause Gate on a grassy path and on to the broad expanse of Maiden Moor, across which a good path leads to the summit of High Spy.

❸ Head down a path towards the col housing Dalehead Tarn. Gradually, the ravine of Tongue Gill appears over to the left, but finding the right moment to quit the Dalehead Tarn path is a hit and miss affair. Such paths as there are across to Tongue Gill are indistinct and invariably wet underfoot, but just keep heading for a fence.

❹ Either of the stiles across the fence gives on to a path leading to a cairn at the start of a path down to Rigghead Quarries. Take care

> **WHILE YOU'RE THERE**
> Consider taking in Castle Crag. The ascent and descent from the main path is clear enough, but it is steep and not suitable for very young children. But what a fabulous viewpoint! To the east, the white-cottaged village of Rosthwaite sits comfortably against a backdrop of hummocky fells and steep crags, while looking northwards you'll see one of the finest views of Derwent Water, the Vale of Keswick and Skiddaw beyond.

> **WHERE TO EAT AND DRINK**
> Grange Bridge Cottage Tea Room in the village of Grange offers a range of teas and snacks throughout the year (reduced opening hours in winter).

descending the steep slate paths until the gradient eases alongside Tongue Gill itself. Keeping to the right bank, follow the gill to a path T-junction, and there turn left to a gate and stile, and footbridge.

❺ The path climbs gently and soon crosses a shallow col near Castle Crag. Go past the crag, descending, soon to enter woodland at a gate. Take a narrow footbridge spanning Broadslack Gill and follow a path down to the banks of the River Derwent. Just before the river, cross a footbridge on the left, and a little further on, keeping to a path roughly parallel with the river until you reach a wall. Take a broad track following the wall and eventually walk out to a surfaced lane. Go right and walk up to Grange village. Go left and follow the road.

❻ Just after Manesty Cottages, branch left on to a path climbing gently above the road to a stile and gate. Through this, go forward on to a gently rising broad track and, when it forks, bear right, heading for a path above an intake wall. This is Point Ⓑ, where Walk 34 rejoins. Pressing on beyond Brackenburn, the footpath, which affords lovely views of Derwent Water, soon dips to make a brief acquaintance with the road at a small quarry car park. Beyond this gap, immediately return to a gently rising path, this is an old road, traversing the lower slopes of Cat Bells that will ultimately bring you back to the road at Hawes End and the car park.

Simply Cat Bells

Shorten the walk and spend more time admiring the views.
See map and information panel for Walk 33

DISTANCE *3.5 miles (5.7km)* MINIMUM TIME *2hrs*
ASCENT/GRADIENT *1,150ft (350m)* ▲▲▲ LEVEL OF DIFFICULTY ✦✦✦

WALK 34 DIRECTIONS
Walk 33 option

Cat Bells is arguably the best known of the lower Lakeland fells: certainly it is one of the most distinctive, its attractive conical shape gracing the western shores of Derwent Water. Many a first step to fell-walking exploration was planted on the grassy slopes of Cat Bells, a summit that remains ever popular for its outstanding views.

The great expanse of Derwent Water lies directly below, while to the north the slate slopes of Skiddaw dominate the market town of Keswick. Further right, the southern ridges of Blencathra overlook Glenderamackin Vale. To the east the Dodds lead into the Helvellyn range, while to the west graceful fells tumble along the skyline from Lord's Seat, across Grisedale Pike and Eel Crags to the high ground above unseen Buttermere beyond Robinson, Hindscarth and Dale Head.

At Point **A**, leave Walk 33 at Hause Gate by turning left on a clear path, and descend a constructed pathway towards the wooded area around Manesty. The path is awkward in places, especially near the top, and lower down broadens into a wide track. Keep descending to meet a path at Point **B** going left along the edge of woodland. (There are two earlier, higher shortcuts that meet this path, though the higher of the two requires care in wet conditions.) Turn left, rejoining Walk 33, and follow the path above the woodland and the attractively set house of Brackenburn.

Brackenburn was the home of Hugh Walpole (1884–1941), the English novelist, born in New Zealand, who bought the property in 1923. His collection of works known as *The Herries Chronicle* (1930–33) is set in and around Borrowdale. Along the path above his home is a bench set before a memorial plaque marking a favoured spot with a stunning view across Derwent Water below.

The northernmost of the lake's islands, Derwent Isle was the base of the German miners who worked in the Newlands Valley during Elizabethan times, and quartered here for their own safety. St Herbert's Island is traditionally the site of a hermitage, and was the inspiration for Owl Island in Beatrix Potter's *The Tale of Squirrel Nutkin* (1903).

Overleaf: Castle Crag and Grange Fell (Walk 33)

Crossroads at Styhead

From Seathwaite to the high mountain pass of Styhead.

DISTANCE 5.75 miles (9.2km)   **MINIMUM TIME** 2hrs 30min

ASCENT/GRADIENT 1,673ft (510m) ▲▲▲   **LEVEL OF DIFFICULTY** +++

PATHS Stony paths and tracks

LANDSCAPE Rugged and mountainous with two high tarns

SUGGESTED MAP OS Explorer OL4 The English Lakes (NW);
6 The English Lakes (SW)

START / FINISH Grid reference: NY 235122 (on Explorer OL 4)

DOG FRIENDLINESS Good for fit, active dogs; under strict control near sheep

PARKING By roadside below farm

PUBLIC TOILETS At Seathwaite Farm

WALK 35 DIRECTIONS

Seathwaite has long been a gateway to the high fells of Lakeland, including Glaramara, Great Gable, and the highest of them all, Scafell Pike. Routes from here lead to the valleys of both Wasdale and Great Langdale. This walk serves to introduce the delights and fascination of the high fells to the ordinary walker. While it doesn't top any of the surrounding heights it does rise to an altitude of some 2,000ft (609m) to view some breathtaking mountain scenery, including the famous tarns of Styhead and Sprinkling. This is technically straightforward, but because of the altitude and the rapidly changing weather conditions you are likely to encounter in the Lakeland fells, everyone

WHERE TO EAT AND DRINK

Passed en route, there is a café at Seathwaite Farm. Light meals are available and there is often a variety of home-made fare.

undertaking this round should be equipped for mountain walking.

Pass through the cobbled farmyard and continue through the gates, along the rough stony track. Once an important packhorse route this ancient highway, known as Styhead Pass, linked Borrowdale to Wasdale, from the heart of mountain Lakeland to the west coast. Along its length travelled illicit wad (a source of locally mined graphite) and whisky to be exchanged for brandy and spices at the ports of Whitehaven and Maryport. Continue to rise to the ancient stone arch of Stockley Bridge which spans Grains Gill. Bear right and cross the bridge. The track, in places reconstructed with pitched stone, continues to ascend the hillside to a gate leading through the stone wall.

Above the wall the way trends right, ascending to skirt the edge of the woods above the ravine of Taylorgill Force. A fence protects the edge and, although the great waterfall is hidden below, it is usually possible to hear its roar. Beyond this point the track follows a line just above the beck to reveal a series of little tumbling falls, rock slides and pools. A little way beyond the point where the going levels, beyond an area of rough stones and boulders, a small wooden footbridge crosses the beck. Take the bridge and continue a few hundred paces to Styhead Tarn. If conditions are favourable this is a good place to take a break and eat your sandwiches.

Traverse above the shore of the tarn then ascend to pass a mountain rescue box to the rough rocky col of Sty Head. This is a famous mountain crossroads and routes from here lead down to Wasdale and up to Scafell Pike, Great Gable and Esk Hause. The tin rescue box contains a stretcher and first aid equipment. It has proved to be a lifesaver on more than one occasion. In extreme weather those caught out in these hills have been known to crawl inside to seek shelter!

WHAT TO LOOK OUT FOR

Small dark red garnets can be found in the rocks of Grains, on the flanks of Seathwaite Fell, above Grains Gill. Classified as a semi-precious gemstone these red crystalline garnets are geologically interesting, though their small size, up to 5mm diameter, makes them worthless in monetary value.

The route lies to the left (east). Follow the stony path along the shoulder. Keep along the main track, ascending to reach the edge of the tear drop known as Sprinkling Tarn. Although sited at an altitude of some 2,000ft (609m), during the summer months its dark surface is often ringed by brown trout jumping

for flies. Keep along the track to pass beneath the dark and foreboding cliffs of Great End. At the half-way point beneath this, a path splits off left. Above this point a great gully cuts directly up the cliff. This is known as Central Gully and in winter, when the westerlies blow snow off the summit plateau of Great End, great accumulations of snow form at its head. As volumes increase the snow becomes unstable and avalanches sweep down the gully. Many an unwary mountaineer has been avalanched out of this gully. Incredibly, fatalities are few and the victims usually escape with broken limbs or cuts and bruises.

WHILE YOU'RE THERE

Behind the farm, to the right of the tumbling waterfalls of Sourmilk Gill, just discernable above a small plantation, are the waste tips of the disused wad mines. Seathwaite wad was once the richest source of graphite, pure carbon, in Europe and these mines were so important that that were protected by armed guard (See Walk 33).

Take the path off to the left (north) and cross the stream to follow the path down the true right bank of Ruddy Gill (leading to Grains Gill). Once very badly eroded this path has now been rebuilt using pitched blocks of rock. Although the descent is steep, and rather hard on the knees, the path is clearly defined: a tremendous achievement by the pathbuilders. It leads over a small footbridge to cross Grains Gill and eventually down to Stockley Bridge. Cross the latter and head back to Seathwaite Farm.

WALK 36

Birkrigg Common's Distant Past

A good outing on Birkrigg Common, strewn with ancient remains.

DISTANCE 8 miles (12.9km) MINIMUM TIME 3hrs

ASCENT/GRADIENT 577ft (176m) ▲▲▲ LEVEL OF DIFFICULTY ✦✦✦

PATHS Paths and tracks, some field paths may be muddy, 10 stiles

LANDSCAPE Low-lying, rolling limestone country, with coastal margin, woodlands, open common and enclosed pastures

SUGGESTED MAP OS Explorer OL6 The English Lakes (SW); OL7 The English Lakes (SE)

START / FINISH Grid reference: SD 301742 (on Explorer OL7)

DOG FRIENDLINESS Under close control on roads and where livestock grazing

PARKING Small car parks between coast road and shore at Bardsea

PUBLIC TOILETS On coast road below village of Bardsea

Birkrigg Common is a wonderful open expanse of bracken, grass and low limestone scars, rising between the shores of Morecambe Bay and the gentle valley containing Urswick Tarn. Although only a lowly height, it offers splendid views encompassing the whole of Morecambe Bay and most of the Furness Peninsula, with Black Combe and the Coniston fells prominently in view. Other Lakeland fell groups, the Yorkshire Dales and Bowland feature more distantly. A network of paths and tracks allow an intimate exploration of the countryside, which turns out to be remarkably varied and interesting.

Geology

The bedrock of Birkrigg Common is Carboniferous limestone. It outcrops only on the margins of the Lake District, most notably around Morecambe Bay and Kendal, but also around Shap and above Pooley Bridge. It was laid down in a shallow sea and once covered the whole of the Lake District, before the area was pushed up into a vast dome by earth movements. Subsequent erosion largely removed the limestone layer, exposing the volcanic core of the Lake District, leaving only a few outcrops of limestone around the fringes.

Birkrigg Common is dry, as most limestone areas are. In the low-lying valley at Urswick, however, water has pooled to form the lovely little reed-fringed Urswick Tarn, which is a haven for waterfowl. Some ground water contained in the limestone layer reaches the surface as freshwater springs out on the sands of Morecambe Bay!

Ancient Settlements

The area around Birkrigg Common was always fairly dry and fertile, compared to the higher Lakeland fells, so it attracted the attention of early settlers. Little remains to be seen, though the most notable feature is an early Bronze-Age small stone circle of limestone boulders on the seaward slopes. A standing stone at Great Urswick, known as the Priapus Stone and thought to be associated with fertility rites, has been forced into a recumbent position at the base of a roadside wall.

BARDSEA

A few tumuli are dotted around the countryside and a rumpled series of low, grassy earthworks represent the remains of an ancient homestead site. Above Great Urswick, a low hill encircled by a limestone scar bears a hill-fort, probably dating from the Iron Age, in the centuries preceding the Roman conquest. It's interesting to wander around and let your imagination run free at the ancient settlement sites. Very little is known about them, but there has been a continual human presence in the area for over 4,000 years.

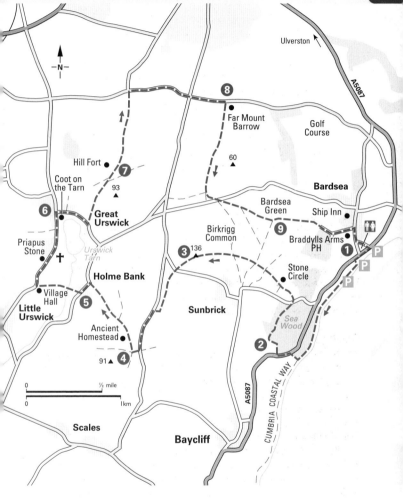

WALK 36 DIRECTIONS

1 Follow the shore along to Sea Wood. At the far end of the wood turn right, up through its inside edge to the road. Turn left up the road for about 400yds (366m), then right at a gate into another part of Sea Wood.

2 Turn left to follow a path around the top edge of the wood, then left again to leave the wood at a gate. Cross a road and follow a grassy path through bracken on Birkrigg Common. Turn left to reach a wall corner and then walk a few paces to a stone circle on your right. Follow any grassy path through the bracken to the high skyline. Birkrigg Common bears a trig point at 446ft (136m) and affords fine views.

3 Pass a bench and take a path to the right down to a road. Cross over and walk parallel to another road as the common tapers out to a cattle grid. Continue along the road and make a sharp right turn along a walled track.

4 Cross a stile at the end of the track and bear right past a stone trough and the site of an ancient homestead. Keep left of a wall to cross a stile at a gate. Bear left to find a path down a valley to a gate. Turn right before the gate, cross a stile, then follow a hedgerow across a slope to a house. Cross a stile leading down to a road, and then turn left to pass farm buildings at Holme Bank.

5 Turn right signposted 'Public Footpath Church Road'. Cross a ladder stile and footbridge, then take a path to a village hall and road. Cross the road and turn right to pass a school. Just after the entrance, the Priapus Stone is incorporated into a wall. Pass the parish church and village store in Great Urswick.

6 Turn right at the Coot on the Tarn to follow another road. Watch for Clint Cottage on the left and Tarn House on the right, then turn left up a steep track.

This is flanked by hedgerows and reaches two gates. Go through the gate on the left and walk straight ahead, keeping right of a low hill; the site of an ancient fort.

7 A wall leads to another gate, then straight on again. Cross a stile on the right, and on the other side of a gate, cross a stile on the left. Walk straight on, crossing two more stiles to reach a road junction. Turn right, walk through a crossroads and to the next farm.

8 Turn right at Far Mount Barrow along a track signposted 'Bardsea Green'. Cross a stile by a gate and keep left to cross a road on Birkrigg Common. Turn left again for Bardsea Green, along an obvious path parallel to the road, then parallel to a wall.

9 At a corner of the wall, go through a gate and follow a track downhill to a road and cross a dip. Keep left at a junction up into Bardsea, then right at the Braddylls Arms and follow a road down to the shore.

In Wordsworth's Footsteps

Follow the poet through Seathwaite and the exquisite Duddon Valley.

DISTANCE 5 miles (8km) **MINIMUM TIME** 3hrs

ASCENT/GRADIENT 850ft (260m) ▲▲▲ **LEVEL OF DIFFICULTY** ✦✦✦

PATHS Paths, tracks, can be muddy below Seathwaite Tarn, 9 stiles

LANDSCAPE Craggy mountainside and wooded gorge

SUGGESTED MAP OS Explorer OL6 The English Lakes (SW)

START / FINISH Grid reference: SD 228960

DOG FRIENDLINESS Can run free through woods at Wallowbarrow

PARKING Roadside pull-off at grid reference SD 231975, limited roadside parking near pub and church

PUBLIC TOILETS None en route

NOTE If River Duddon in spate, not advisable to cross at Fickle Steps Point ❺. Return to Seathwaite along road instead

---

On loitering Muse — the swift Stream chides us — on!
Albeit his deep-worn channel doth immure
Objects immense portrayed in miniature,
Wild shapes for many a strange comparison!
Niagaras, Alpine passes and anon
Abodes of Naiads, calm abysses pure
Bright liquid mansions, fashioned to endure
When the broad oak drops a leafless skeleton,
And the solidities of mortal pride,
Palace and tower, are crumbled into dust! —
The Bard who talks with Duddon for his guide,
Shall find such toys of fancy thickly set:
Turn from the sight, enamoured muse — we must;
And, if thou canst, leave them without regret!

William Wordsworth (*Hints for the Fancy from The River Duddon*, 1820)

Williiam Wordsworth loved the Duddon Valley so much that he wrote many such sonnets about it. And little has changed since his day. There's tarmac on those winding walled lanes, but the byres and woods and the lively stream that so enthralled the poet are still there for all to see.

The walk begins in Seathwaite, a remote village with a rustic pub, a little church and a handful of farms, set beneath the crags of Wallowbarrow. A reservoir service road takes the route easily up into the Coniston fells to the dam of Seathwaite Tarn. The large reservoir is dwarfed by the rocks of Grey Friar and Buzzard Crag towering above. On some days it's an uninspiring place and needs a little help from evening light or, as on the occasion when I last visited, a dull windless day when the sulking crags were reflected to perfection in the hushed and gloomy waters.

DUNNERDALE

Look the other way though and the landscape needs no help, especially if the bracken glows red to blend with the dusky heather, the crags and the odd lonely pine. The jagged cone of Harter Fell dominates the skyline high above the forests, streams and farmhouses. Our route descends through the heather and the bracken, and by a chattering beck to the Duddon. Over the road, it comes to the Fickle Steps across the river. Wordsworth remembers them in a fanciful sonnet:

> *Not so that Pair whose youthful spirits dance*
> *With Prompt emotion urging them to pass;*
> *A sweet confusion checks the Shepherd lass;*
> *Blushing she eyes the dizzy flood askance;*
> *Too ashamed — too timid to advance*

There's a wire across the river to steady your progress these days. It's an exciting prelude to a wonderful walk through the Wallowbarrow Gorge. From a lofty path you look down on the river and it's bounding cataracts, then descend for a riverside stroll back into Seathwaite.

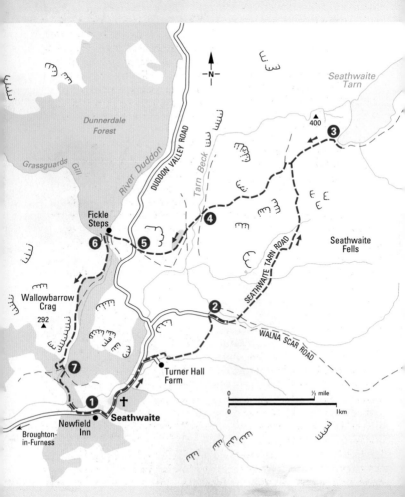

DUNNERDALE

WALK 37 DIRECTIONS

1 From the Newfield Inn at Seathwaite in Dunnerdale follow the main valley road past the little church, then turn right on the tarmac lane towards Turner Hall Farm. Leave this and follow a track on the left through a gate marked 'High Moss'. Where the track ends, keep to the left-hand side of the farm, go through the top gate and follow the field path out to the Walna Scar Road.

2 Turn right along the road, then left on to the utility company's access road to Seathwaite Tarn. This pleasant track climbs steadily to the reservoir dam.

3 Retrace your steps for around 200 paces to a waymarking post highlighting a downhill path that weaves through rock and rough pasture. Crossing over a tiny beck it continues down to a gate, leading to a boggy field. On the far side of this, another gate leads to a ladder stile on the right.

4 Cross the stile and footbridge over Tarn Beck. On the opposite bank turn left and follow an obvious, wet, path through a gate and on along the edge of a wood. Pass behind a lovely cottage and continue in the wood past a barn on the left until the path rises to enter open country. Continue on this marshy way to the road.

5 Across the road follow the signed bridleway to the Fickle Steps, huge boulders, which allow you to cross the River Duddon. (Caution: if the river is in spate here and the steps are underwater, return by the road.)

6 To continue on the route, turn left, go over the footbridge across Grassguards Gill, then climb along a waymarked path above the tight wooded Wallowbarrow Gorge. The footpath descends again to cross boulder-strewn terrain on the bank of the River Duddon.

7 When you reach a tall one-arched footbridge, cross over to the other side of the river and turn right along the path, now tracing the eastern bank of the Duddon. Go over the footbridge spanning a tributary, Tarn Beck, before following a path out to the road. Turn left to walk back to your car in Seathwaite village.

From Eskdale to Miterdale

Discovering peaceful hills that were once a Norman hunting preserve.

DISTANCE 6.75 miles (10.9km)   **MINIMUM TIME** 4hrs

ASCENT/GRADIENT 1,312ft (400m) ▲▲▲   **LEVEL OF DIFFICULTY** +++

PATHS *Good paths in valleys, but often indistinct on hills, 4 stiles*

LANDSCAPE *Heath and moor with views across surrounding valleys*

SUGGESTED MAP *OS Explorer OL6 The English Lakes (SW)*

START / FINISH *Grid reference: NY 173007*

DOG FRIENDLINESS *On lead as sheep roam moors*

PARKING *Car park beside Dalegarth Station (pay-and-display)*

PUBLIC TOILETS *At Dalegarth Station*

NOTE *Walk not advised in poor visibility*

Although William the Conqueror arrived in England in 1066, much of the North remained controlled by the Scots, and it was not until William II took Carlisle in 1092 that Norman influence spread through Lakeland. Some settlement was encouraged and land granted to found monastic houses, but much of the mountainous area remained undeveloped. The main reason for this lay in the Normans' almost fanatical devotion to the hunt, an activity, exclusively reserved for the King and a few favoured subjects. Vast tracts of this northern 'wasteland' were 'afforested', not in today's sense with the planting of trees, but set aside as wild game reserves and subject to special regulation, the Forest Law.

The area around Eskdale lay within the barony of Copeland, a name which derives from the Old Norse 'kaupaland' meaning 'bought land', and was granted to William de Briquessart in the early 12th century. His forest, together with the neighbouring Derwentfells Forest, extended all the way from the Esk to the Derwent and remained under Forest Law for more than a century. The forest was not devoid of settlement, but the few peasants who lived within its bounds were subject to many draconian laws that affected almost every aspect of their meagre existence. The clearance of additional land for grazing or cultivation, known as 'assarting', was forbidden and it was illegal to allow cattle or sheep to stray into the forest. Felling a tree for timber to repair a cottage or fencing required special permission and even the collection of wood for fuel was strictly controlled.

The estate was policed by foresters, who were keen to bring malefactors before the forest courts for punishment. The penalties were often severe ranging from a complex system of fines for minor infringements to flogging, mutilation or even death for poaching. Often near to starvation themselves, the commoners were required to assist as beaters, butchers and carriers for the hunts, and watch their overlords kill, perhaps, more than 100 deer in a single day. Yet if game animals broke through the fences around their allotments and destroyed the paltry crop, they were powerless to do anything other than chase them away. The hunting preserve gradually diminished during the 13th century, as larger areas were turned over to sheep farming, and constant nibbling has prevented the regeneration of natural woodland and left the open landscape now so characteristic of the area.

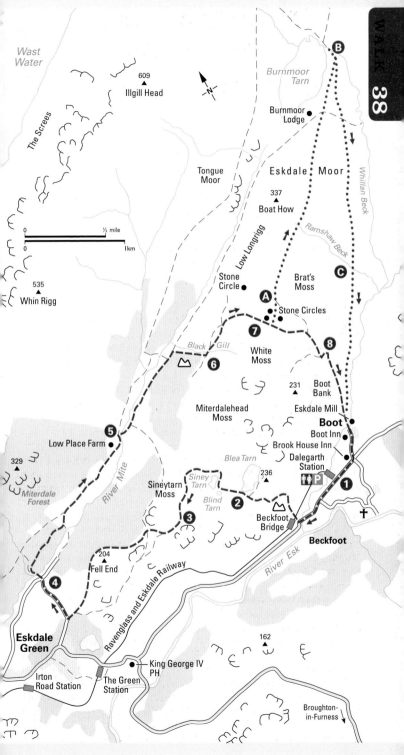

Wast Water

The Screes

609 ▲
Illgill Head

Burnmoor Tarn

Burnmoor Lodge

Eskdale   Moor

Tongue Moor

Whillan Beck

337 ▲
Boat How

Ramshaw Beck

Low Longrigg

Stone Circle ●

Ⓐ

Brat's Moss

Ⓒ

535 ▲
Whin Rigg

Stone Circles ●●

⑦

White Moss

Black Gill

△ ⑥

⑧

231 ▲
Boot Bank

Miterdalehead Moss

Eskdale Mill

Boot

Low Place Farm ●

⑤

Boot Inn

Brook House Inn

329 ▲

River Mite

Blea Tarn

Dalegarth Station

Miterdale Forest

Sineytarn Moss

Siney Tarn

236 ▲

🅿

①

③

Blind Tarn

②

△

Beckfoot Bridge

Beckfoot

River Esk

✝

204 ▲
Fell End

④

Ravenglass and Eskdale Railway

Eskdale Green

162 ▲

King George IV PH ●

Irton Road Station

The Green Station

Broughton-in-Furness

WALK 38 DIRECTIONS

1 Follow the lane down the valley towards Beckfoot Bridge. Immediately before the railway halt, cross the line to a gate from where a zig-zag path to Blea Tarn is signed up the hillside. Approaching the tarn, go left crossing a stream.

WHERE TO EAT AND DRINK

There is a café at Dalegarth Station, but if you want something more substantial, call at either the Boot Inn or the Brook House Inn, in Boot.

2 A vague path maintains the firm ground, right of Blind and Siney tarns, then, at a fork, bear left. Beyond a lone tree, go left again. The way is marshy around Sineytarn Moss but a dry route can be found. Eventually, the route joins a wall, dropping beside it to level grass.

WHILE YOU'RE THERE

A watermill still stands beside the packhorse bridge in Boot. It was built to grind corn in 1578 and worked by successive generations of the same family for almost 350 years. The mill has since been restored and is now open as a fascinating museum.

3 Bear right to a fence stile by a forest and continue along its edge below Fell End. Keep going near the wall, reaching its corner in about 0.75 mile (1.2km). A short track on the right descends to a junction, and another right turn takes you into Miterdale.

4 Emerge on to a tarmac lane at the bottom and go through a gate opposite into Miterdale Forest. Drop over the river and then bear right on an undulating, weaving path above its far bank. A lateral wall shortly forces you uphill on to a forest track. Turn right and follow it out of the trees, joining a track from the right to continue up the valley to Low Place farm.

5 Walk past the farmhouse and through a second yard, leaving by the right-hand gates, signed 'Wasdale'. Follow the river upstream before crossing a bridge to a track that continues along its opposite bank. Keep ahead for nearly 0.75 mile (1.2km) until you cross a stile at the far end of a plantation. Here, leave the track and climb the hill beside the trees to another stile at the top.

6 Bear left above Black Gill and continue parallel to a wall towards the higher ground of Low Longrigg. After 400yds (366m) strike right on a barely visible path, making for the stone circles, which briefly break the horizon.

7 Bear right at the second circle and, after passing beneath a rocky outcrop, fork left. The way is still vague, but now drops towards stone huts where a clear path descends by them to the right.

8 Follow it down Boot Bank and into Boot, and cross Whillan Beck by Eskdale Mill to continue through the village. At the end turn right to Dalegarth Station.

WHAT TO LOOK OUT FOR

Scattered across Brat's Moss are the remains of stone huts and a field system as well as five impressive circles of standing stones. They were erected during the Bronze Age, perhaps 5,500 years ago, and suggest quite a large settlement on what is now an almost desolate landscape.

On to Burnmoor Tarn

Wander on below Boat How to Burnmoor Tarn, dramatically sited below the western shoulder of Sca Fell.
See map and information panel for Walk 38

DISTANCE *10 miles (16.1km)* **MINIMUM TIME** *5hrs*
ASCENT/GRADIENT *1,575ft (480m)* ▲▲▲ **LEVEL OF DIFFICULTY** +++
NOTE *Not advised in poor visibility*

WALK 39 DIRECTIONS
(Walk 38 option)

Follow the instructions for Walk 38 as far as Point **7**, but where the path divides at the second stone circle, branch left. After cresting a low rise, you will meet a track climbing across Brat's Moss from the right, Point **A**.

The way ahead is clear, undulating easily across the south-western flank of Boat How. Beyond the hill, the route gradually loses height but, not until you begin to think that the pool has disappeared, does Burnmoor Tarn burst into view. Keep going above the shore past a lonely, but surprisingly substantial cottage, Burnmoor Lodge, until you reach the foot of the tarn, where Whillan Beck is born, Point **B**.

The return route leaves from the head of Whillan Beck, but instead of retracing your outward steps, fork left on to a path, which initially runs parallel. Just beyond a cairn, bear left, but then keep ahead a little further on, ignoring a path that drops to the stream. Shortly after crossing Ramshaw Beck, Point **C**, the way passes through a gate to leave the open fell. Continue ahead along the edge of successive rough enclosures, intermittently accompanied by a wall on the left. Eventually, through a gate, rejoin the main walk, which falls from the right into Boot.

Although there has long been a chapel at Wasdale Head, it was not licensed for burials until the 19th century. Consequently, when a villager died, the body had to be taken to the parish church, St Catherine's, at Boot. The corpses were carried over the lonely pass between the two valleys, beside Burnmoor Tarn and then down to the village along the track above Whillan Beck, the Coffin Road. On one occasion, the party must have set out late, for they were still high on Eskdale Moor when night closed in and an enveloping mist rolled down from the surrounding fells. For some reason, the horse, carrying the body strapped to its back, suddenly bolted into the darkness and neither were seen again. So, take care to reach the village before nightfall, for it is said that the horse can sometimes be heard after dark, galloping across the moor still burdened with its gruesome load.

Whinlatter Forest Park

A high mountain forest combines gentle trails and strenuous fell walking.

DISTANCE 5 miles (8km)	**MINIMUM TIME** 4hrs
ASCENT/GRADIENT 662ft (202m) ▲▲▲	**LEVEL OF DIFFICULTY** ✦✦✦
PATHS Good paths and tracks, some rough walking, 2 stiles	
LANDSCAPE Forest, fells and lakes	
SUGGESTED MAP OS Explorer OL4 The English Lakes (NW)	
START / FINISH Grid reference: NY 208245	
DOG FRIENDLINESS Off lead provided they're under control	
PARKING Reasonably priced parking at Visitor Centre	
PUBLIC TOILETS At Visitor Centre	

WALK 40 DIRECTIONS

Whinlatter Forest is a mixed plantation of trees ranging from Sitka and Norway spruce to Scots pine, Douglas fir and Lawson cypress. Look out also for native broadleaves such as birch and oak and the more exotic western hemlock and Japanese larch. The forest provides a habitat for a wide range of wildlife and on this walk you may see roe deer, red squirrels, frogs, toads and foxes. Badgers live here too but, unless you are very lucky, the nearest you'll get to them is the reconstruction of a scaled-up badger set next to the Visitor Centre. It's great for kids and even adults enjoy walking through it and imagining what life must be like as a badger.

Overhead you may see buzzards, peregrines and many other species of bird life. One species you do have a good chance of seeing, depending on the time of the year, is the osprey. For the first time in over 150 years a breeding pair of ospreys has nested in England. The huge nest, built by the Forestry Commission and the Lake District National Park Authority, is located in Thornthwaite Forest and is subject to a round-the-clock guard once the female lays her eggs.

Ospreys have a wingspan of nearly 5ft (1.5m) and are rich brown in colour with a white head and underside. They're fish eaters and you are most likely to see one hovering over Bassenthwaite Lake, its sharp eyes scanning the water for a fish before transforming itself into a feathered missile streaking down unerringly to spear its prey.

WHAT TO LOOK OUT FOR

Why not have a bash at orienteering? Revlin Moss at the foot of Grisedale Pike is the home of Europe's first permanent trail orienteering course. Following gravel paths the Revlin Moss Trail has some of the easiest walking in the area. People in wheelchairs, the very young, and anyone not up to the more strenuous walks can still enjoy spectacular views of Grisedale Pike from this trail.

Ospreys winter in Africa, but return to the Lake District in the spring to breed.

The walk begins from the badger set beside the Visitor Centre following a series of way-marked trails to a viewpoint. To begin with follow the coloured markers up the hill. Turn left with the green markers to a T-junction. Turn left again to Horsebox Crossroads and the number 2 marker post. This is another great viewpoint with the dramatic ridge of Grisedale Pike rising in front of you and the smaller, Hobcarton End to the right. Turn right here and continue along the forest road until it makes a U-turn. Turn right on to a path marked by post 24, then head uphill through the forest on to the fellside to another T-junction close to post 5. Turn left and keep on the path as it climbs uphill and over a stile to the summit of Lord's Seat.

On a clear day you should be able to see the Solway Firth and the hills of the Scottish Southern Uplands as well as the high Lakeland fells to the south and east.

Leave the summit by following the well-worn path on the east side and head downhill before climbing again to the summit of Barf. Below you and stretching away

to the right is the Vale of Keswick with Derwent Water, dotted with islands, beyond. There's also a grand view over Bassenthwaite Lake and this is probably your best chance of spotting the ospreys. Just across the water from here is Dodd Wood where there is an osprey viewing point. It's staffed and there are telescopes and binoculars available from late June through to the end of August, from 10am to 5pm. The site is open during the rest of the year but you will have supply your own binoculars. You will find the viewing area near the Dodd Wood car park.

Start heading back downhill keeping the Vale of Keswick to your left. Turn right and take care on the steep path. Cross Beckstones Gill and go over a stile into Beckstones Plantation. Turn left down the track, passing marker post number 21 and a path leading downhill to the left, and keep going on the wide track until you reach a T-junction. Turn left on to the forest road, follow it to another T-junction, turn right and continue for 440yds (402m) to a fork. Go left and downhill along a well-defined path. Pass through a deer fence and turn left, downhill when you, when you meet the red waymarker. Follow these back to the Visitor Centre car park.

Overleaf: Stone circle at Swinside near Duddon Bridge (Walk 41)

Count the Stones at Swinside

Discover Swinside Stone Circle hiding in a hollow above the Duddon.

W A L K

41

DISTANCE 6 miles (9.7km)   **MINIMUM TIME** 2hrs 30min

ASCENT/GRADIENT 820ft (250m) ▲▲▲   **LEVEL OF DIFFICULTY** ✦✦✦

PATHS Good paths, some can be muddy, farm roads, 6 stiles

LANDSCAPE Wooded slopes, mostly rough pasture surrounded by hills

SUGGESTED MAP OS Explorer OL6 The English Lakes (SW)

START / FINISH Grid reference: SD 197882

DOG FRIENDLINESS On lead where sheep graze and on roads

PARKING Parking space at Duddon Iron Furnace, near Duddon Bridge

PUBLIC TOILETS None en route; nearest at Broughton-in-Furness

NOTE If Black Back is in spate, stepping stones are uncrossable
and the detour adds 0.75 mile (1.2km)

This is a quiet walk in one of the quietest corners of the Lake District. Most of the people you meet around the Duddon Valley have travelled no great distance; local folk have a high regard for its hidden delights. The walk stretches almost all the way from a tidal estuary to the flanks of the high fells, taking in old coppice woodlands and pastures where sheep and cattle are grazed.

Blast furnaces and charcoal burners once belched smoke into the clean air, and ships laden with pig iron sailed from the narrow estuary, but that was a couple of centuries ago. Tucked away in a natural amphitheatre in the hills, and seldom visited, Swinside Stone Circle has stood over the scene for 4,000 years or more.

Duddon Iron Furnace

Dating from 1736, the Duddon Iron Furnace was one of eight rural blast furnaces in the area. Apart from the addition of an extra charcoal store, the structure has hardly changed from the day it was built. Information boards show the layout of the site, which included charcoal and iron ore stores, a wheelhouse, furnace, blowing house, casting house, office and slag heap. Ore and charcoal were fed into the furnace from the top of the site and pig iron left at the bottom. Ships sailing out of the Duddon Estuary transported the iron to Bristol and Chepstow for use in the shipbuilding industry. The small rural furnaces simply went out of business when bigger blast furnaces were constructed. The ruins are managed by English Heritage and are always open for inspection.

Swinside Stone Circle

The lovely Swinside Stone Circle sits in a quiet hollow in the hills high above the estuary of the River Duddon. It is a late neolithic or early Bronze Age structure, with its stones closely packed together. It appears to be aligned on the Midwinter solstice and is about 95ft (29m) in diameter. Locally it is called 'Sunkenkirk'; the name being drawn from a legend relating how a church was once being built on the site, but the Devil kept pulling the stones down into the ground. Like many

DUDDON BRIDGE

such circles around the country, it is also said that anyone counting the stones more than once will find that they arrive at a different number each time. With that in mind, it's probably best to say that there are over 50, but less than 60 stones in the circle! There is also a series of standing stones near Ash House towards the end of the walk, but there is no public access to them.

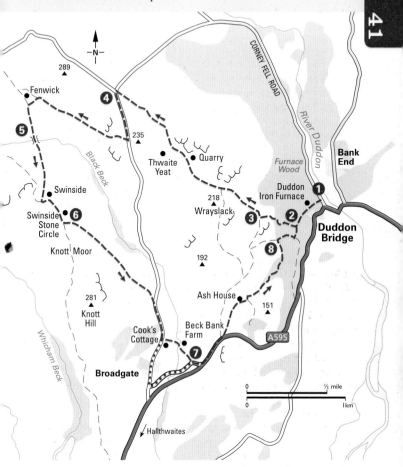

WALK 41 DIRECTIONS

❶ The Duddon Iron Furnace is on the left of the Corney Fell road, soon after the turning from Duddon Bridge. A public bridleway sign points up a track beside the ruins. At the last building, turn left up a woodland path marked by a bridleway sign hidden among brambles.

❷ Cross a narrow access road and continue uphill. Turn right at a junction and keep climbing. A track is joined leading further up the wooded slope, but watch for a gate in a wall on the left. Go through and follow a deep, narrow path flanked by bracken, crossing a low gap in the hills.

❸ Turn right to reach a gate. Go through and follow a walled track. When another gate is reached, go through and turn left. A path running roughly parallel to a tall wall passes an old quarry near a farm called Thwaite Yeat. The path is vague on a moorland slope, but look ahead to spot a signpost at a road junction.

❹ Turn left down a narrow road signposted 'Millom', and then turn right along a farm track. It crosses a dip and leads to a gate marked 'Fenwick'. Go through and follow the track almost to the farm, but turn left as indicated by a public footpath sign. Cross three stiles as the path leads down through fields to Black Beck.

❺ Cross a footbridge and climb uphill, looking ahead to spot Swinside farm. Keep to the right of the buildings, but turn left to join and follow the access road away from the buildings. Swinside Stone Circle is in a field on the left.

❻ Walk down the farm access road and continue along a tarmac road to Cook's Cottage. Just before the building is a stile and public footpath signpost. A field path and stile lead to Black Beck and stepping stones lead to Beck Bank Farm. Two tracks lead from the farm to a nearby road. Use the one on the left. If the stones are uncrossable, retrace your steps to Cook's Cottage and turn left down the road, through Broadgate to a T-junction. Turn left, along

the road past old mill buildings to rejoin the route at Point 7.

❼ Turn left along the road and left again along a busy main road. Walk round a bend to find two farm roads signposted as public bridleways. Take the second one to Ash House. Leave the garden through a gate and turn left, over a stile. Turn right, by the fence along a narrow path. Another stile leads into woods. Walk uphill, then down to reach a marker post at a junction.

❽ Turn right and walk downhill, then turn left at a junction. Keep right at another junction, following a path that was used earlier. Cross a narrow access road and walk down to the Duddon Iron Furnace and the start of the walk.

Commanding Black Combe

Climb out on a limb, far removed from the higher Lakeland fells.

DISTANCE 8.5miles (13.7km)   **MINIMUM TIME** 4hrs

ASCENT/GRADIENT 1,883ft (574m) ▲▲▲ **LEVEL OF DIFFICULTY** +++

PATHS Clear path to top, rather vague beyond, no stiles

LANDSCAPE Broad, open, whaleback hill covered in bracken and heather

SUGGESTED MAP OS Explorer OL6 The English Lakes (SW)

START / FINISH Grid reference: SD 136827

DOG FRIENDLINESS On lead or under close control on grazing land and on road

PARKING Car park at Whicham church or lay-by at Whitbeck church

PUBLIC TOILETS None en route; nearest at Silecroft beach

NOTE Not advised in poor visibility

Black Combe truly dominates this quiet corner of the Lake District. Its steep slopes rise to a domed summit that often wears a woolly cap of cloud. Moist air rising from the Irish Sea has to cross Black Combe before reaching the higher fells, so tends to leave a puffy cloud tethered to the summit as water vapour starts to condense. Bear this in mind when attempting to climb the fell; the whole idea is to enjoy the view from Lakeland's last fell and cloud cover will confound the plan. Also bear in mind that this is one of the higher and more remote walks in the book. Black Combe is not a place to be caught out in foul weather.

William Wordsworth commented on the view from Black Combe, claiming that 'the amplest range of unobstructed prospect may be seen that British ground commands' though lamenting, 'we have seen into Scotland, Wales, the Isle of Man… but alas we have still failed to see Ireland as we have been promised'. He seems to have been drawing on comments made by the 18th-century surveyor Colonel Mudge, who said that the summit offered a more extensive view than any other point in Britain. Mudge was lucky enough to see Ireland several times, though only before sunrise and after sunset.

Black Combe is made of friable Skiddaw slate, which outcrops, naturally, around Skiddaw and also on the Isle of Man. It is the oldest exposed rock in the Lake District, belonging to the Ordovician period of 450–500 million years ago and weathers to produce domed summits covered in patchy scree and thin, poor soil. Bracken covers the lower slopes of the fell, giving way to bilberry and heather on the higher slopes, though the summit is a delightful swathe of short green grass. Tree cover is sparse and confined to the lower slopes. Grouse, introduced for sport, flourish on the slopes along with snipe and the ubiquitous curlew.

Several streams have carved deep little valleys in the flanks of Black Combe. Whit Beck was once used to turn a waterwheel at Whitbeck Mill. The present building, restored as a dwelling, dates from the 18th century, though may stand on an earlier mill site. The dilapidated wheel last turned in 1916. Too many old farms and cottages lie derelict or disused on the flanks of the hill, victims of wavering farm economies, and Black Combe is one large sheep-grazing range today.

BLACK COMBE

↑ Bootle

Butcher's Breast

⌂

● Sheepfold

Hallfoss Beck **5**

Hall Foss ●

6

Little Fell

Holegill Beck

A595

● Fell Cottage

Monkfoss Beck

⌂

4

600 Black Combe

587 ▲

Millergill Beck

⌂

Whitbeck Mill

Whitbeck

Townend Hall †

Townend Gill

Townend Knotts

3

Haligill Beck

Pen End

A595

⌂

Parsonage Breast

7

CUMBRIA COASTAL WAY

2

Parsonage Farm

Kirkbank **1** P †

A595

Whicham

A5093

Station

Silecroft

Miner's Arms PH ●

↓ Kirksanton, Millom

0 ½ mile
0 1km

—N—

BLACK COMBE

WALK 42 DIRECTIONS

1 Leave the car park at Whicham church and follow a short path to a lane. Turn left to walk up, behind Kirkbank on a good track. At a corner of a wall, turn right up a path and through a gate on to the slopes of Black Combe.

2 The fellside is covered in bracken, but a broad, grassy path leads straight up a little valley. Avoid a path to the left. Towards the top of the valley, bracken gives way to grass and bilberry. Looking back, coastal views are developing nicely, stretching beyond Millom to the Furness Peninsula.

3 The broad path becomes stony as it slices up across a heathery slope, levelling out as it approaches the summit. In mist, watch carefully for a sudden right turn on to the broad, domed top of Black Combe. A trig point is enclosed by a circular wall at 1,970ft (600m).

4 You can turn around and retrace your steps to Whicham, or enjoy a fine circuit around the fell. Head north from the summit to join a path onwards. Turn left downhill at a small cairn. The path, flanked by tussocky grass and heather, can be vague in places.

5 Swing left just before an old sheepfold. The path is firm and grassy. Keep left at a fork for a steep descent, or right for a gentler descent. Either way, the path later swings left and

continues down beside a fence on Butcher's Breast. The village in view below is Bootle. The path runs beside a wall, fords Hallfoss Beck and passes close to the ruined farm of Hall Foss.

6 Keep to the path beside the wall, fording Holegill Beck near a solitary larch. Pass abandoned Fell Cottage and cross Monkfoss Beck. When a fork is reached, keep left to follow a grassy path across a slope of bracken. A track leads past Whitbeck Mill, continues past the buildings that constitute Whitbeck, and then reaches the main road at Whitbeck church.

7 Turn left along the main road, walking on the right for safety. Maps mark a path parallel to the road, but this is overgrown. Follow the road until a wooden footpath sign points left up a slope. The path climbs beside a wall, and then runs gently down to a track. The track passes Kirkbank and leads on to the narrow lane followed at the start. A short path on the right leads back to Whicham church.

Around Buttermere

A relaxing walk in one of Lakeland's most attractive valleys.

DISTANCE *4.5 miles (7.2km)*   MINIMUM TIME *2hrs*

ASCENT/GRADIENT *35ft (11m)* ▲▲▲ LEVEL OF DIFFICULTY +++

PATHS *Good path, some road walking, 2 stiles*

LANDSCAPE *Lake, fells, woodland and farmland*

SUGGESTED MAP *OS Explorer OL4 The English Lakes (NW)*

START / FINISH *Grid reference: NY 173169*

DOG FRIENDLINESS *On lead near farms and open fells where sheep are grazing*

PARKING *National Park car park beyond Fish Hotel (fee)*

PUBLIC TOILETS *At start*

Much has been written about Buttermere, the dale, the village and the lake. And it remains, as it has been since Victorian times, a popular place displaying 'nature's art for art's sake', as W G Collingwood described it in *The Lake Counties* (1902). Nicholas Size's historical romance, *The Secret Valley* (1930), takes a rather different and much earlier line, describing a tale of guerrilla warfare and bloody battles here with invading Norman forces.

Buttermere, however, achieved considerable notoriety at the pen of Joseph Budworth, who stayed here in 1792 and encountered Mary, the daughter of the landlord of the Fish Inn. In his guidebook *Fortnight's Ramble to the Lakes*, he describes Mary as 'the reigning Lily of the Valley' and began what must have been a reign of terror for Mary, who became a tourist attraction, a situation made worse in later editions of Budworth's book, in which he revelled in the discomfort all the unwanted attention heaped on Mary and her family.

More sinisterly, in 1802, the tale brought to Buttermere one John Hadfield, a man posing as the Honourable Anthony Augustus Hope MP. Hadfield wooed and won Mary, and they were married at Lorton church on 2 October 1802 (coincidentally just two days before William Wordsworth married Mary Hutchinson). With the honeymoon scarcely begun, Hadfield was exposed as an impostor, and arrested on a charge of forgery – a more serious offence than of bigamy, of which he was also guilty – and later tried and hanged at Carlisle. Accounts of the whole episode are given by Thomas de Quincey in *Recollections of the Lakes and the Lake Poets* and by Melvyn Bragg in his 1987 novel *The Maid of Buttermere*, a description used by Wordsworth in *The Prelude*. The whole saga was dramatised and found its way on to the stages of some London theatres. Happily for Mary, she later remarried, had a large family and by all accounts a happy life.

With such a backcloth, it is something of an intrigue that in a Victorian satire of 1851, by Henry Mayhew, generously entitled *The Adventures of Mr and Mrs Cursty Sandboys and Family*, who came up to London to 'Enjoy Themselves' and to see the Great Exhibition, Buttermere is described as the quietest and most secluded of Lakeland villages, where '…the knock of the dun never startles the hermit or the student – for (thrice blessed spot!) there are no knockers'.

BUTTERMERE

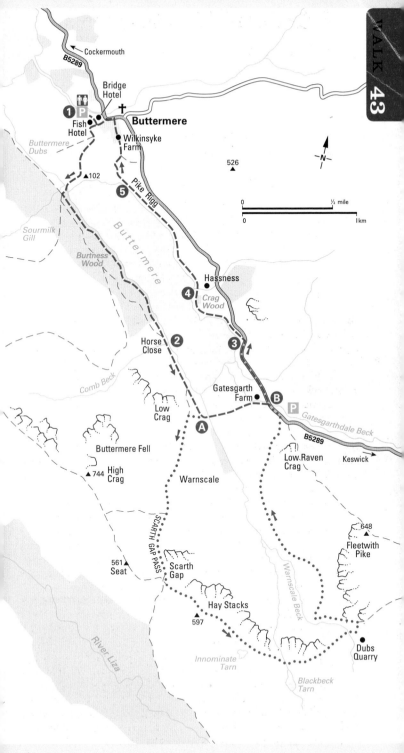

Cockermouth

B5289

Bridge Hotel
Buttermere
Fish Hotel
Wilkinsyke Farm
Buttermere Dubs
▲102
Pike Rigg
Sourmilk Gill
Burtness Wood
Buttermere
Hassness
Crag Wood
Horse Close
Comb Beck
Low Crag
Gatesgarth Farm
Gatesgarthdale Beck
B5289
Keswick
Low Raven Crag
Buttermere Fell
▲744 High Crag
Warnscale
Warnscale Beck
.648
Fleetwith Pike
SCARTH GAP PASS
561▲ Seat
Scarth Gap
Hay Stacks
▲597
Dubs Quarry
River Liza
Innominate Tarn
Blackbeck Tarn

526 ▲

0   ½ mile
0   1km

WALK 43 DIRECTIONS

W A L K 43

1 Leave the car park and turn right, passing the Fish Hotel to follow a broad track through gates. Ignore the signposted route to Scale Force and continue along the track towards the edge of the lake. Then follow the line of a hedgerow to a bridge at Buttermere Dubs. Cross a small footbridge and go through a nearby gate in a wall at the foot of Burtness Wood and the cascade of Sourmilk Gill. Turn left on a track through the woodland that roughly parallels the lakeshore, finally emerging from the woodland near Horse Close, where a bridge spans Comb Beck.

2 Keep on along the path to reach a wall leading to a sheepfold and a gate. This is Point **A**, where Walk 44 branches off. Go left through the gate, cross Warnscale Beck and walk out to Gatesgarth Farm. At the farm, follow the signs to reach the valley road. This is Point **B**, where Walk 44 rejoins. A short stretch of road walking, left on the B5289, now follows, along which there are no pathways. Take care against approaching traffic.

3 As the road bends left, leave it for a lakeside footpath on the left. The path leads into a field, beyond which it never strays far from the shoreline and continues to a stand of Scots pine, near Crag Wood.

4 Beyond Hassnesshow Beck bridge, the path enters the grounds of Hassness, where a rocky path, enclosed by trees, leads to a gate. Here a path has been cut across a crag where it plunges into the lake below, and shortly disappears into a brief, low and damp tunnel, the only one of its kind in the Lake District. The tunnel was cut by employees of George Benson, a 19th-century mill owner who owned the Hassness Estate, so that he could walk around the lake without straying far from its shore. After you emerge from the tunnel a gate gives access to a gravel path across the wooded pasture of Pike Rigg. A path leads through a series of gates beyond the foot of the lake to a bridge of slate slabs.

5 A short way on, through another gate, the path leads on to Wilkinsyke Farm, and an easy walk out to the road, just a short way above the Bridge Hotel. Turn left to return to the car park.

Hay Stacks

Extend the walk with a tour across the rocky delights of Hay Stacks.
See map and information panel for Walk 43

DISTANCE *8 miles (12.9km)*   **MINIMUM TIME** *4hrs*
ASCENT/GRADIENT *1,673ft (510m)* ▲▲▲   **LEVEL OF DIFFICULTY** +++
PATHS *Rocky fell paths, some mild hands-on scrambling, 1 stile*

WALK 44 DIRECTIONS
(Walk 43 option)

More than any other fell in Lakeland, Hay Stacks demonstrates how mere height can often be given an elevation it doesn't deserve. Surrounded by higher fells, this modest summit displays qualities many other fells lack. It boasts dramatic perches, superb vistas (one that many rank among the best ten in the Lake District), rocky knolls, heathery hollows, peat bogs, pretty tarns – even a summit tarn – winding trails and hidden corners. It was rightly described by Alfred Wainwright, whose ashes were scattered on Innominate Tarn, as '…a place of great charm and fairyland attractiveness'.

At Point Ⓐ, turn right on to a rocky path rising alongside a small plantation. At a fence corner go left. (This point can also be reached by leaving the Buttermere path just before the end of the lake by branching right on to a stony path.) Continue alongside the plantation and then begin a long, delightful and steady ascent of what used to be the old packhorse track linking Buttermere with Ennerdale and then by Black Sail Pass into Mosedale and Wasdale. At the top of the pass, known as Scarth Gap, turn left at a large cairn, not far from rusted fence stanchions, and tackle a series of easy rocky interludes (you will need to use your hands). Finally, just beyond a small tarn, you reach the summit, a neat ridge with cairns at either end.

From the top, head off on a clear, descending path that makes first for Innominate Tarn and a lovely rocky passage leading to the outflow of Blackbeck Tarn. Cross Black Beck, climbing briefly before making a cross-country trek descending towards the spoil and buildings of Dubs Quarry.

The path crosses Warnscale Beck and turns left, contouring the fell slope to intercept a more pronounced and broad track. Turn left on to this and follow its course all the way into Warnscale Bottom, descending through one of the most awesome mountain corries in Lakeland, rugged, craggy and wild.

At the foot of Warnscale, the path continues easily to meet the road at Gatesgarth Farm. Turn here left to join Walk 43 at Point Ⓑ.

Nether Wasdale

This walk takes in some of the delights of Cumbria's deepest lake, most magnificent screes and prettiest woods.

DISTANCE 4.5 miles (7.2km)   **MINIMUM TIME** 2hrs 30min

ASCENT/GRADIENT 165ft (50m) ▲▲▲   **LEVEL OF DIFFICULTY** ✦✦✦

PATHS Well-defined paths and farm tracks, 7 stiles

LANDSCAPE Farm pasture, deciduous woodland, low moor

SUGGESTED MAP OS Explorer OL6 The English Lakes (SW)

START / FINISH Grid reference: NY 128038

DOG FRIENDLINESS Can run free in Low Wood, on lead elsewhere

PARKING Verges of road triangle east of Nether Wasdale village

PUBLIC TOILETS None en route

WALK 45 DIRECTIONS

If you're driving past Nether Wasdale, chances are you're on the way to Wasdale Head, and thinking about the climb to Great Gable, or England's highest mountain, Scafell Pike. Nether Wasdale and its surrounding oak woods are pretty, but these narrow, twisting lanes and their enclosing stone walls make you concentrate on your driving. But Nether Wasdale's too good to be dismissed. Delightful paths through those oak woods lead to the Wast Water, where you can look across to the expansive steel-cold screes that fan out from murky and mysterious gullies in Whin Rigg's rockfaces.

From the triangle take the southbound Santon Bridge road, which straddles the River Irt on a stone bridge. Just beyond the bridge by Flass House, turn left, following a farm track signed 'Wast Water'. The track leads through fields to Easthwaite Farm. Go through the farmyard and continue along the track through more fields, but now tucked beneath the rocks of Irton Fell. Keep on the main track, ignoring a right fork beyond the farm. After joining a riverside path by Low Wood the track reaches the Wast Water Pumphouse at the southern tip of Wast Water. Water from the lake is pumped from here to the nuclear plant at Sellafield.

As lakes go Wast Water is fairly sterile. When water tumbles down the impervious volcanic rocks of the surrounding mountains, few of the minerals needed for a rich cycle of life are leached out into the lake. You'll see some black-headed gulls and maybe the occasional red-breasted merganser duck on an excursion from the salt marshes of the Irt Estuary, but the most fascinating visitor to

WHERE TO EAT AND DRINK

The welcoming Strands Hotel is a typically English country inn with low beams and a real fire to warm you on a winter's evening. It's a free house with guest beers and a wide range of bar meals.

NETHER WASDALE

Wast Water is a fish. The Arctic char comes here to spawn in the lake's ice-cold waters each year between November and March, and has been doing so since the last Ice Age.

Beyond the pumphouse a narrow, undulating path traces the lakeshore to reach the great fans of boulder known as the Wast Water Screes. This is a fragile environment, but the purple saxifrage grows in the gullies, as does the more common alpine lady's mantle, a dwarf plant with tiny yellow-green flowers.

WHAT TO LOOK OUT FOR

Take a look round Gosforth village. In St Mary's churchyard is a 14ft (4m) ancient cross, the highest of its kind in England. The cross has pagan Viking symbols on one side and Christian engravings on the other.

Retrace your steps, to Low Wood. Here a waymarked path follows the field edge by the Irt to Lund Bridge where you cross over, into the woods. A path now winds through the trees, bends left behind a little boathouse and continues with the lakeshore to the right. The leafy path weaves through oak, beech and birch. Winter greenery is added by the odd yew and holly bush. Unfortunately, there are also rhododendrons. Introduced from Asia, this fast-growing shrub has quickly adapted itself to the countryside, particularly woodland. Here its dense foliage blocks out light and prevents other plants from taking root.

The path joins a wider track, which descends from the left. Continue to follow it by the riverside. On the left you'll see

Wasdale Hall, a magnificent mansion, now used as a youth hostel – ignore paths to it. Beyond a ladder stile over a wall the path climbs out to the Wasdale Head road. Here, you get a grand view over the lake towards the screes, Yewbarrow and Great Gable.

Turn left along the road then, after about 300yds (274m), turn right along a wide stony track through High Birkhow Woods, passing to the left of Wasdale Hall's walled gardens. Go over a stile at the end of the track to enter high pastures with the crags of Buckbarrow and Middle Fell ahead.

The path begins as a faint grooved track, heading half left across the pastures towards a small crag. From here it becomes well defined and winds downhill to meet a bridleway. Turn left to follow the grassy bridleway, which aims south-west with the rocks of Ashness How to your left. You could make a short there-and-back detour to see Woodhow Tarn.

Otherwise continue straight ahead over another stile to follow a track that passes a cottage before veering left to the Nether Wasdale road. Turn right, back to the triangle.

WHILE YOU'RE THERE

Peregrines nest on the cliff edges and precipitous crags around Buckbarrow. This medium-sized falcon is distinctive with its wingtops and upper body flecked with various shades of grey. Its cheeks are white, and its lower body, pale with dark grey streaks. The peregrine's unbelievably good eyesight allows it to see prey from 2 miles (3.2km) away. When it finds something, the bird dives at great speed from the sky and with talons outstretched towards its unfortunate victim.

Getting High on Lonely Loweswater

Discovering Lakeland's finest balcony in a peaceful and little-trodden corner of the north-western fells.

DISTANCE 5 miles (8km) **MINIMUM TIME** 3hrs

ASCENT/GRADIENT 650ft (200m) ▲▲▲ **LEVEL OF DIFFICULTY** ✦✦✦

PATHS Well-defined paths and tracks, all stiles have adjacent gates

LANDSCAPE Hillside, farm pastures, forest and lakes

SUGGESTED MAP OS Explorer OL4 The English Lakes (NW)

START / FINISH Grid reference: NY 134210

DOG FRIENDLINESS On lead, except for Holme Wood

PARKING Maggie's Bridge car park, Loweswater (get there early)

PUBLIC TOILETS None on route

Loweswater is one of Lakeland's finest yet least talked about lakes; perhaps because it's a bit remote from the more popular parts of Lakeland. 'Where's Loweswater then?' some people will ask. Well, it's that lake beyond Buttermere and Crummock Water; the one you never quite got around to visiting because you were awed by the beauty of the other lakes. The fellwalker judges Lakeland by the height of the fells, and the fells here are low – one's even called Low Fell. But somehow, standing on the lakeshore, it doesn't matter.

Loweswater's a bit of a thief: it steals the best views of Crummock Water's fells – Grasmoor and Whiteside never looked more fair than they do from Carling Knott's balcony path, and little Mellbreak bursts into the sky like a volcano – with its steep and rocky slopes.

Following the Corpse Road

Loweswater village is little more than the Kirkstile Inn, the church and the village hall, with a scattering of whitewashed farm buildings in the lush green fields and alongside the narrow country lanes. The walk starts on the outskirts of the village, by Maggie's Bridge. It uses an old corpse road to get to the fellsides. The corpses? They would have been parishioners from Loweswater, for the church didn't have its own burial ground. They would be strapped on to horses' backs before being carried all the way to St Bees on the coast. After the climb up the high sides of Carling Knott, the mourners might not have appreciated that this is one of the most splendid balcony paths in Cumbria – green, flat and true – and with wonderful views across the lake to Darling Fell.

To Farmland and Lake

The old track descends to farm pastures. The names of the farmhouses, Iredale Place, Jenkinson Place and Hudson Place, are all derived from the original owners' names. Beyond the last-mentioned, the route drops to the lake. Loweswater is celebrated among anglers for its trout and its perch. Both fish are hunted down by the predatory pike, a huge streamlined fish present here in large numbers.

The path continues into the National Trust's Holme Wood. Oak predominates near the lake, although the trees at the top of the wood largely consist of pine, larch and Sitka spruce. The wood is one of the last strongholds of the red squirrel. You're very likely to see pied and spotted flycatchers here, and maybe, if you're lucky, a green woodpecker.

The path, leaves the lake behind, comes out of the woods and crosses the fields of Watergate, back to Maggie's Bridge. Mellbreak still towers above the trees, tauntingly, tantalisingly showing off its scree paths to the summit. Another day perhaps, for this has been a day for quiet contemplation.

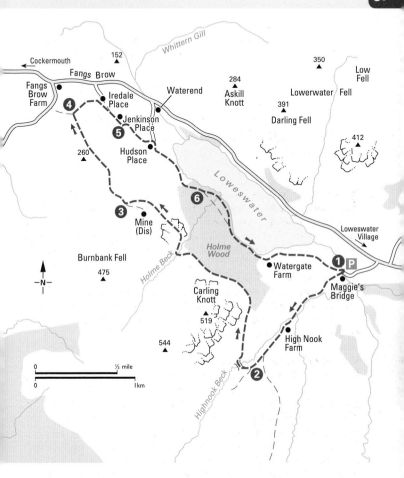

WALK 46 DIRECTIONS

1 Just opposite the car park entrance go through the gate to High Nook Farm and follow the track through the fields. After passing through the farmyard continue along a stony track that climbs into the comb of Highnook Beck and beneath the craggy sides of Carling Knott.

2 Take the right fork each time the path divides. This will bring you down to the footbridge across the beck. Across the bridge the route continues as a fine grassy track that doubles back right, raking across the hillside to the top of the Holme Wood plantations. The track follows the top edge of the woods before traversing the breast of Burnbank Fell.

WALK 46

❸ The track swings left and climbs to a ladder stile and a gate to the north of the fell. Here it divides. Ignore the left fork, which doubles back to an old mine. Instead go over the stile and descend gradually north-west across high pastureland.

❹ A couple of hundred paces short of the road, at Fangs Brow, turn right over a ladder stile and then continue along a rutted track past Iredale Place farm. Just beyond the house the track joins a tarmac lane.

❺ Beyond Jenkinson Place (a farm) the tarmac lane ends. Turn left here, over a stile and follow a well-defined grass track across the fields towards Hudson Place and the lake. A signpost diverts the way left, around the

farm complex. The path meets a lane from Waterend farm. Turn right and follow the lane, which becomes a track near the shores of Loweswater before entering Holme Wood.

❻ A wide track now heads through the woods, but by taking a path to the left, you can get nearer the shoreline. This second path rejoins the original track just beyond a stone built bunkhouse. At Watergate Farm, turn left to follow a wide gravel road back to the car park at Maggie's Bridge.

Discovering Nannycatch

A fine walk on the edge of Lakeland taking in one of Cumbria's lovely secret valleys.

DISTANCE 9.25 miles (14.9km)   MINIMUM TIME 5hrs

ASCENT/GRADIENT 1,378ft (420m) ▲▲▲   LEVEL OF DIFFICULTY +++

PATHS Well-defined paths and tracks with 5 stiles

LANDSCAPE Lake and riverside pastures, forest and moorland

SUGGESTED MAP OS Explorer OL4 The English Lakes (NW)

START / FINISH Grid reference: NY 012130

DOG FRIENDLINESS Can run free through forest

PARKING Free car park at Longlands Lake, Cleator

PUBLIC TOILETS None en route; nearest at main car park in Egremont

Cleator, Cleator Moor, Frizington, Rowrah – they're all rather gloomy places with rows of 19th-century terraced housing and telephone wires dangling across the street. This is where the last hills of Cumbria decline to the Ehen Valley, and, as forestry cloaks the slopes, it looks as though there's nothing to keep the walker here. Yet those who've done Alfred Wainwright's Coast to Coast walk, from nearby St Bees to Robin Hood's Bay in North Yorkshire, know different. They've seen what lies beyond the first hill; the hidden valley and the clear, crystal stream that dances through it. They've seen Nannycatch!

Before the 1780s Cleator Moor was just that – a moor, untouched and windswept. But not far beneath those grasses were veins rich in haematite, a red iron ore and the growing need for high-quality iron started a rush to equal that of the Klondyke. The Longlands Mine at Cleator first produced iron ore in 1879. Flooding from the River Ehen was always a problem and by 1924 the last pit closed. By the start of the Second World War, continued subsidence caused the flooding of the area now known as Longlands Lake. Cumbria County Council bought the site in 1980 and have added the footpaths at the start of the walk.

After taking the circular trip around the lake, the route follows the banks of the Ehen before climbing on Wainwright's Coast to Coast walk through forests of pine and spruce. The path finally breaks free on the hilltop of Dent where it marches through wind-bent rushes, mosses and moor grass to a cairn with a surprise view. Beyond the pale rounded hump of Lank Rigg the skyline is filled with Lakeland peaks, from Grasmoor and High Stile to the mighty crags of Sca Fell and Scafell Pike.

But it's Nannycatch you've come to see, and you only get glimpses from here. Its beauty becomes evident when seen from the steep grassy hill slopes east of the forest. It's hard to believe this little stream has cut such a deep craggy valley, but Nannycatch has a secret: when an ice sheet from the last ice age blocked what is now the Ehen Valley, it was Nannycatch Beck that drained Ennerdale. Once in the valley you'll be struck by the steep-sided, gorse-covered slopes topped by hanging crags and screes. You'll vow to return; maybe when the gorse flowers, when the bracken dries to crinkly red, or when the grass is frosty and icicles hang from streamside boulders.

200 ▲

Nannycatch Gate

Lowther Park

Nannycatch Beck

Raven Crag

290 ▲

272 ▲

Meadley Reservoir

Flat Fell

283

5

Kirk Beck

Uldale

6

352 ▲

180 ▲

Uldale Plantation

Dent

4

NANNYCATCH ROAD

Ennerdale Bridge

Longbarrow Moss

252 ▲

Cow Field

Roughton Beck

Black Beck

Wath Bridge

B5295

3

Blackhow Wood

←N—

Cleator Moor

Black How

A5086

84 ▲

Egremont

2

Blackhow Bridge

Cleator

Longlands Lake

P

1

River Ehen

0 ½ mile

0 1km

WALK 47 DIRECTIONS

1 Go over the suspension bridge at the back of the car park and turn right along the circular path around Longlands Lake. Back at the bridge, follow the east bank of the Ehen to Blackhow Bridge.

2 Turn right along a winding, unsurfaced lane. Just beyond Black How farm turn right, cross a road, and go through the gate opposite to follow a forestry track uphill through the conifers of the Blackhow Wood.

3 Leave the track for a waymarked path on the left, then, at another waymark, turn right to follow a forest ride up the hill. At the top of the plantation the path follows a fence to the pile of rocks marking the west summit.

4 Follow the hilltop path over the next top, then down a cleared area of Uldale Plantation. Where the path meets a narrow forest track, turn left, then left again along a wider track. Watch out for a stile in a clearing on the right – this gives you access to the open fell and that view of Nannycatch.

5 Although many still use the direct path down into Nannycatch, the landowner wants you to go back along the wide forestry track past the Coast to Coast

waymarker, and to turn left at a crossroads, and continues along a grassy track that zig-zags down steep slopes into Uldale.

6 Turn left along the forestry road you meet in Uldale, and cross Kirk Beck, before turning left through a gate. Recross Kirk Beck and follow the bridleway upstream to Nannycatch Gate. After going through a gate just beyond Raven Crag, ignore the public bridleway on the left, and instead continue alongside Nannycatch Beck.

7 Double back to the left, up a well-defined track heading west on the northern flanks of Flat Fell. The path veers left across the grassy slopes to reach the Nannycatch Road. Follow the road downhill and turn left along a quiet lane at the near side of Wath Bridge. When you get to Black How farm, retrace your steps back to the car park, by the side of Longlands Lake.

Overleaf: Cannon on the terrace at Muncaster Castle (Walk 48)

Over Muncaster Fell

A fine linear walk from Ravenglass to Eskdale Green, returning on La'al Ratty.

DISTANCE 6 miles (9.7km) **MINIMUM TIME** 2hrs 30min

ASCENT/GRADIENT 730ft (220m) ▲▲▲ **LEVEL OF DIFFICULTY** ✚✚✛

PATHS Clear tracks and paths, muddy after rain, 1 stile

LANDSCAPE Woodlands, moderately rugged fell and gentle valley

SUGGESTED MAP OS Explorer OL6 The English Lakes (SW)

START Grid reference: SD 085964

FINISH Grid reference: SD 145998

DOG FRIENDLINESS Under close control where sheep are grazing

PARKING Village car park at Ravenglass, close to station

PUBLIC TOILETS Ravenglass village and Ravenglass and Eskdale Station

Muncaster Fell is a long and knobbly fell of no great height. The summit rises to 758ft (231m), but is a little off the route described. A winding path negotiates the fell from end to end and this can be linked with other paths and tracks to offer a fine walk from Ravenglass to Eskdale Green. It's a linear walk, but when the Ravenglass and Eskdale Railway is in full steam, a ride back on the train is simply a joy. It's also possible to return to Ravenglass using the optional extension, Walk 49.

Affectionately known as La'al Ratty, the Ravenglass and Eskdale Railway has a history of fits and starts. It was originally opened as a standard gauge track in 1875 to serve a granite quarry and was converted to narrow gauge between 1915 and 1917. After a period of closure it was bought by enthusiasts in 1960, overhauled and re-opened, and is now a firm favourite. The line runs from Ravenglass to Dalegarth Station, near Boot at the head of Eskdale. The railway runs almost all year, but there are times in the winter when there are no services. Obtain a timetable and study it carefully. When the trains are running, there are few Lakeland journeys to compare with a trip both ways.

The Romans operated an important port facility at Ravenglass. Fortifications were built all the way around the Cumbrian coast to link with Hadrian's Wall and a Roman road cut through Eskdale, over the passes to Ambleside, then along the crest of High Street to link with the road network near Penrith. Some people think the Romans planned to invade Ireland from Ravenglass, though this is a subject of debate. The mainline railway sliced through the old Roman fort in 1850, leaving only the bathouse intact, though even this ruin is among the tallest Roman remains in Britain. The Romans also operated a tileworks on the lower slopes of Muncaster Fell and the site is passed on Walk 49.

Surrounded by luxuriant rhododendrons, Muncaster Castle is almost completely hidden from view. It has been the home of the Pennington family since about 1240, though they occupied a nearby site even earlier than that. The estate around the castle includes a church that was founded in 1170, as well as a network of paths and tracks to explore. Owls are bred and reared at Muncaster, then released into the wild.

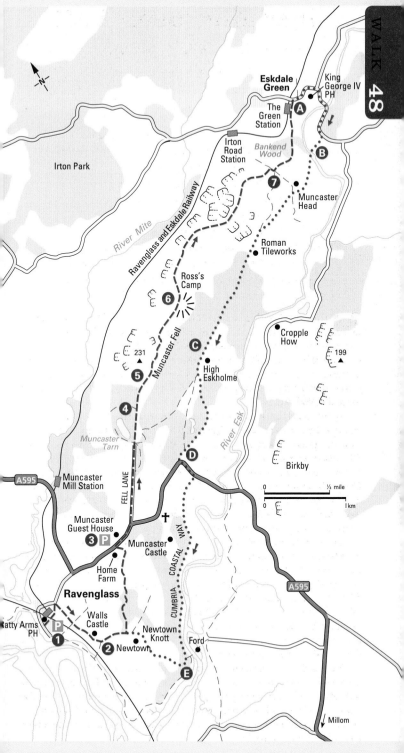

WALK 48 DIRECTIONS

❶ Leave the car park by crossing the mainline and miniature railway line, using the footbridges, then follow a narrow path to a road junction. Turn right on a footpath by the side of a narrow road, signposted 'Walls Castle'. The bathouse is soon on the left.

WHILE YOU'RE THERE

Don't forget to explore the little village of Ravenglass. It's essentially a fishing village at the confluence of the rivers Irt, Mite and Esk. Apart from being a Roman port, by 1280 it had charters for a weekly market and annual fair, though its trade was eclipsed as the port of Whitehaven developed and it became a rum-smuggling centre.

❷ Continue along the access road and turn left along a track signposted 'Newtown'. Turn left again before the cottage and follow another track up a little wooded valley. Go through four gates, following the track from the wood, across fields and into another wood. Turn left to reach Home Farm and a busy main road.

❸ Cross the road and turn right, passing Muncaster Castle car park and the Muncaster Guest House. The road leads up to a bend, where Fell Lane is signposted uphill. Ascend the clear track, cross a little wooded dip, then fork right and left, noticing

WHERE TO EAT AND DRINK

The Ratty Arms is in the old mainline railway station at Ravenglass. Families are welcome and meals are serveded. The King George IV is near The Green Station and offers over 100 malt whiskies, food and lodgings.

WHAT TO LOOK OUT FOR

The Ravenglass estuary is a haunt of wildfowl and waders. Oystercatchers and curlews probe the mudflats and there are sometimes raucous gulls. On Muncaster Fell there may be grouse in the heather and it's usual to see buzzards overhead.

Muncaster Tarn on the left. Go through a gate at the top of the lane to reach Muncaster Fell.

❹ A path forges through boggy patches along the edge of a coniferous plantation, then the path runs free across the slopes of Muncaster Fell. A path rising to the left leads to the summit, otherwise keep right to continue.

❺ Views develop as the path winds about on the slope overlooking Eskdale. A panorama of fells opens up as a curious structure is reached at Ross's Camp. Here, a large stone slab was turned into a picnic table for a shooting party in 1883.

❻ Continue along the footpath, looping round a broad and boggy area to reach a corner of a dry-stone wall. Go down through a gateway and bear in mind that the path can be muddy. There is a short ascent on a well-buttressed stretch, then the descent continues on a sparsely wooded slope, through a gate, ending on a track near another gate.

❼ Go through the gate and then turn left, crossing a field to reach a stone wall seen at the edge of Bankend Wood. Walk on keeping to the right side of the wall to reach a stile and a stream. A narrow track continues, becoming better as it draws close to a road. Turn left at the end of the road to reach The Green Station.

Down the Dale to the Sea

Extend Walk 48 with an easy route through beautiful Eskdale to return to Ravenglass.
See map and information panel for Walk 48

DISTANCE *13 miles (20.9km)* **MINIMUM TIME** *4hrs 30min*
ASCENT/GRADIENT *787ft (240m)* ▲▲▲ **LEVEL OF DIFFICULTY** +++

WALK 49 DIRECTIONS
(Walk 48 option)

If there are no trains running back to Ravenglass, or if you just want a longer walk, then here's an easy route back to the sea. A good track leads along the lower slopes of Muncaster Fell, passing the site of an old Roman tileworks and a private golf course. The route links tracks and paths passing close to Muncaster Castle and its owl centre, weaving around the wooded estate and alongside the tidal reaches of the River Esk. The latter parts of the walk can be muddy in wet weather.

Walk from The Green Station, Point **Ⓐ**, down the road to the King George IV pub. Turn right at a junction and follow the road across the River Esk. Then, turn right along an access road signposted 'Muncaster Head Farm'. The road crosses a stone bridge, dated 1889, spanning the River Esk, Point **Ⓑ**.

After passing Muncaster Head Farm, there are two gates where the track forks. Keep to the right and follow the track into forest where some parts have been felled and replanted. The Romans operated a tileworks to the left of the track. Reach an open area at High Eskholme, where there is a private golf course, Point **Ⓒ**.

Shortly after passing High Eskholme, a sign points left through a gateway, indicating a public bridleway across the golf course. Walk alongside a strip of forest, through a gate, then along a clearer track. When a gate gives way to a broader track, turn right and follow it past a house and up to the busy main road, Point **Ⓓ**.

Turn left down the main road, then right at a gatehouse to follow a clear track across fields. A Cumbria Coastal Way signpost points left inside a woodland fence. (A diversion is signposted when herons are nesting.) Go through a gate and cross a footbridge, following a woodland path up to a track. Turn left down the track and walk beside the River Esk to reach a set of tide tables near a ford, Point **Ⓔ**.

Just beyond the tide tables, turn right away from the river through a gate. Walk uphill through another gate in a wall, then follow a track to the left of Newtown Knott. It leads to a gate at Newtown Cottage, then it's simply a matter of retracing your earlier steps of the day back to Walls Castle and Ravenglass.

Dramatic St Bees Head

The high sandstone cliffs of St Bees make a formidable bastion against the Irish Sea.

WALK 50

DISTANCE 3.25 miles (5.3km) **MINIMUM TIME** 2hrs 15min

ASCENT/GRADIENT 460ft (140m) ▲▲▲ **LEVEL OF DIFFICULTY** ✦✦✦

PATHS Track, grassy paths and lane, 11 stiles

LANDSCAPE Elevated fields, rocky bay, cliff top and open seascapes

SUGGESTED MAP OS Explorer 303 Whitehaven & Workington

START / FINISH Grid reference: NX 948146

DOG FRIENDLINESS Good for fit and active dogs under strict control

PARKING Tarnflatt Hall by private access road to lighthouse, small fee payable at farmhouse

PUBLIC TOILETS On seafront at St Bees village

WALK 50 DIRECTIONS

This walk makes a strenuous, though rewarding, round of the North Head of St Bees. North Head forms an imposing headland of sandstone looking out across the Irish Sea to the Isle of Man and over the Solway to the hills of Galloway in Scotland.

Here you'll find the most spectacular sea cliffs in the north-west of England, home to an important nesting colony of seabirds. The cliff top is largely owned by the Royal Society for the Protection of Birds (RSPB) and this route will be most interesting in the spring and summer months, when the birds are in residence. Even so, the autumnal and winter gales can provide their own attractions. When huge breakers roll over Fleswick Bay to smash against the cliffs this becomes very much a walk on the wild side.

From the parking area within the farmyard return to the surfaced road and walk back along to the top of the hill marked by the telecommunications mast. Take the track on the right, Hannahmoor Lane, signed 'Coastal Way – Fleswick Bay'. Proceed through the gate and continue along the track, dipping at first and then rising, to climb the shoulder of Hannah Moor. Keep along the track crossing four stiles and gates. There are grand views east to the Lakeland fells and west across to the Isle of Man.

The fourth stile has waymark arrows showing the path to fall diagonally down the next open field. There is no obvious worn path. Perhaps the draughtsmen who drew the green right of way had a slip of hand here and it may be prudent to cross the field directly before descending right, down the line of the far boundary. About half-way down the slope a post marks where a stile, once crossed a vanished fence. Exit the field by another stile at the bottom. Go right to a stile leading over the fence and follow the

ST BEES

path and steps down into the little ravine. Near its base a path bears off to the left and leads out through the mouth of the canyon to the delights of Fleswick Bay. A natural sun-trap, and a popular sunbathing and swimming facility for the hardy natives of west Cumbria, this bay is a wonderful place to watch birds.

Return to the path and continue. Cross a stile and, beyond this, cross the little stream to skirt back left along a slippery shelf of sandstone. A further stile leads out on to the open hillside and the steep path, with sections of steps, rises to the cliff top. There are fine views across Fleswick Bay to the cliffs of the South Head. Follow the path along the fence which runs close to the cliff edge. Cross two stiles. At intervals stiles over the boundary fence provide access to safe viewing areas.

These viewing areas, built by the RSPB and maintained by a seasonal warden, offer an opportunity to inspect the noisy bird life nesting on the cliffs below. Many thousands of birds return here each spring to lay their eggs and hatch their chicks before returning to sea where they spend three-quarters of their lives. Most prolific are the guillemots, which resemble dumpy little penguins. Some 5,000 of these birds squeeze precariously on to the narrow open ledges. Razorbills, not so common, can also be seen here along with fulmars, gulls and some 1,600 pairs of kittiwakes.

Just beyond the second stile along the top, a pinnacle flake of rock can be seen. The gap isn't far, though the rift is very deep. Named Cloven Barth on the map this feature is known locally as Lawson's Leap after a character who thought, fatally, he could make the jump across. A little way beyond this, on intercepting a concrete road just before a white building with a little square tower, go right, up to the lighthouse. The first lighthouse here was built by Thomas Lutwige c1723. It consisted of a round tower of some 30ft (9m) in height, supporting a large metal grate on which coal was burnt. It lasted until 1822 and earned the considerable accolade of being the last coal-fired lighthouse in use in Great Britain.

Pass the lighthouse, taking the gate which leads on to the road, and continue back to Tarnflatt Hall.

Walking in Safety

All these walks are suitable for any reasonably fit person, but less experienced walkers should try the easier walks first. Route finding is usually straightforward, but you will find that an Ordnance Survey map is a useful addition to the route maps and descriptions.

RISKS

Although each walk here has been researched with a view to minimising the risks to the walkers who follow its route, no walk in the countryside can be considered to be completely free from risk. Walking in the outdoors will always require a degree of common sense and judgement to ensure that it is as safe as possible.

- Be particularly careful on cliff paths and in upland terrain, where the consequences of a slip can be very serious.

- Remember to check tidal conditions before walking on the seashore.

- Some sections of route are by, or cross, busy roads. Take care and remember traffic is a danger even on minor country lanes.

- Be careful around farmyard machinery and livestock, especially if you have children with you.

- Be aware of the consequences of changes in the weather and check the forecast before you set out. Carry spare clothing and a torch if you are walking in the winter months. Remember the weather can change very quickly at any time of the year, and in moorland and heathland areas, mist and fog can make route finding much harder. Don't set out in these conditions unless you are confident of your navigation skills in poor visibility. In summer remember to take account of the heat and sun; wear a hat and carry spare water.

- On walks away from centres of population you should carry a whistle and survival bag. If you do have an accident requiring the emergency services, make a note of your position as accurately as possible and dial 999.

COUNTRYSIDE CODE

- Be safe, plan ahead and follow any signs.

- Leave gates and property as you find them.

- Protect plants and animals and take your litter home.

- Keep dogs under close control.

- Consider other people.

For more information visit www.countrysideaccess.gov.uk/things_to_know/countryside_code